ONCE A MAN – TWICE A BOY

ONCE A

Man

TWICE A

Boy

MEMORIES OF A BEDFORDSHIRE FARMER

CLAUDE BANKS

Matador
9 Priory Business Park
Kibworth Beauchamp
Leicestershire LE8 0RX, UK
Tel: (+44) 116 279 2299
Fax: (+44) 116 279 2277
Email: books@troubador.co.uk
Web: www.troubador.co.uk/matador

ISBN 978-1783065-387

British Library Cataloguing in Publication Data.
A catalogue record for this book is available from the British Library.

Typeset in Aldine by Troubador Publishing Ltd
Printed and bound in the UK by TJ International, Padstow, Cornwall

Matador is an imprint of Troubador Publishing Ltd

I dedicate this book to

My beloved grandmother, Kate Banks (nee Reynolds)

My Wife, Daphne

My Children, Penny, Sally and Jamie

My grandchildren, Louise, Tristan, Alexander and Harry

My great grandsons, Edward, Albert and Henry

I feel that history has come full circle as these small great-grandsons like nothing more than to sit on my knee and help to 'drive' my truck around the farm, just as I, as a very small boy, was allowed to take the reins of Grandfather's (horse drawn) buggy all those years ago.

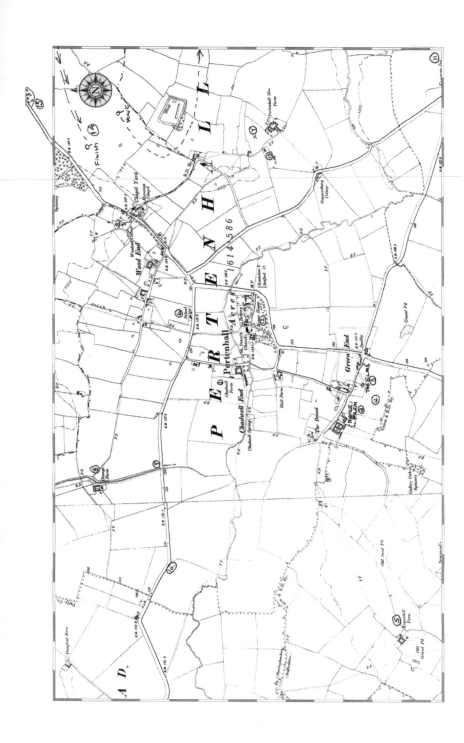

Key to Map

1. Chadwell Farm (Claude was born here)
2. Manor Farm (Claude's Grandparents lived here)
3. The Elms (Aunts and Great Aunts lived here)
4. The Cricket Field
5. Middle Lodge (where Dr.Kilby delivered the baby in a snowstorm)
6. Pertenhall Primary School
7. Cottage which burnt down in August 1931 (mentioned in a story)
8. Shelton's Farm (where the Italian prisoner-of-war was shot)
9. The brook where the little girl drowned in 1950
10. The field where the bullocks were taken from, to Bedford Market, to fund the trip to the gold rush.
11. The Kangaroo Inn
12. The Manor – home of General Loch – Head of Pertenhall Branch of the Home-Guard
13. Bunny Reynolds home
14. The Racecourse – see the start and finish line
15. The Straw Stacks in the story "fun and games"

Contents

Local characters

Life is Like That

Village Life

Foreword

Every rural community has its own local 'knowledge' interwoven into the combined memories of its inhabitants. As a relative newcomer (twelve years a Kimbolton resident is but a 'brief encounter') and a historian at heart, piecing together that fabric is both a need and a pleasure. In my first years 'up at the Castle' I was introduced to a kaleidoscope of names. All too often I had no chronology to thread together these seemingly disparate characters. And then it all began to click. *"So X was Y's grandson and used to live in that house, so they were neighbours of the Zs, the ones who suffered that harrowing tragedy. What tragedy? When? Where? "* And, again, I would be left in that fog of ignorance which stalks the newcomer.

If anyone can piece together the jigsaw, Claude Banks is the man. Pertenhall and Kimbolton are ever-present keystones to his life and the characters who flit in and out, the backdrop to a life well-lived. From the loss of his mother, before the forming of even the most nascent of memories, through the positive influence of his grandmother, to the key events of the 20th Century, viewed through the prism of rural Huntingdonshire (yes, and Bedfordshire too); it's all here, the characters, farming through the decades and, of course, Kimbolton School – or 'the old Grammar School'. The Castle/School association was not even a gleam in the Headmaster's eye when Claude was a pupil. The ravages of war put paid to huge swathes of English class and rural privilege, sweeping the Duke of Manchester from Katharine of Aragon's old home and paving the way for Kimbolton School to move up the road. Generations of pupils, and a Headmaster or two, have proved the ultimate beneficiaries.

Despite my professional interest in the School, my attention was particularly rapt by the chapter on local cricket. As a present-day playing member of Kimbolton Cricket Club, at the close of play (possibly with pint in hand) I always enjoy casting my eye over the old team photographs hanging in the Pavilion. Claude brings a number of these old timers back to life, just as he does so many other characters and events over the succeeding pages; like me, enjoy.

Jonathan Belbin
Headmaster, Kimbolton School (2002 –)

Kate Banks nee Reynolds – Claude's paternal grandmother

Acknowledgements

My first stories were published in the Parish Magazine, but they were soon reaching a wider audience, when a magazine covering some 30 local villages was launched and my contributions quickly went from bi-monthly to monthly, by popular demand.

Although my memory has enabled me to write my stories, I have been indebted to three ladies who have been able to decipher my scrawl and type them up, namely Kath Brittain, Joyce Shrubbs (who as Joyce Taylor was one of my old flames at Pertenhall Primary School back in the 1930's) and finally Gwennan Owen who has also helped rush through the final stories to beat the publisher's deadline.

I have also been indebted to so many people who have provided information regarding dates and verifying facts and at the risk of missing someone's name, may I thank all who have contributed in any way. The one person I will mention, who sadly is not with us any more is Bunny (Albert) Reynolds, because his memory totally eclipsed mine and his help on many occasions was invaluable.

To all my family, especially Daphne my long suffering wife and Penny our eldest daughter who is the driving force in getting the book published.

Finally to Helen Hopperton in the Old Kimboltonian's Office and the Headmaster, Jonathon Belbin, not only for kindly writing the forward to the book but for also arranging for the book to be launched at the Old Kimboltonians Reunion Day.

My Life Story

I have enjoyed writing my stories and anecdotes for The Bystander and I have had many requests for these to be compiled into a book, so I have handed this task over to our eldest daughter, Penny, whilst I continue with the 'Tales from a time gone by' production line! Having read quite a few autobiographies, in my time, I would like this book to be less about me, but more about friends and acquaintances, whose company I have enjoyed over the years.

Briefly, readers might like to know my background, and whether I was found under a gooseberry bush or delivered by stork to Chadwell Farm Pertenhall on January 25th 1926! The first thing I can remember was being carried up the stairs by my Grandmother at Manor Farm and told to kneel down beside the bed and say my prayers then being tucked in she sang "Twinkle twinkle little Star" until I went to sleep. Later on I was to learn it was on Boxing Day 1928 that my mother had passed away earlier in the day. The amazing thing is that I can remember nothing about my mother and looking at her photo, it seems as though she could have been a complete stranger.

The next year was spent playing with my toys in the "big" house and going round the farm with grandfather in his (horse-drawn) buggy and occasionally down to the farm at Stonely to check on the livestock and on to Kimbolton to the bank.

I started at Pertenhall Church of England School at four years of age in the infants' class of about ten boys and girls, the teacher was Miss Kate Cook from Hoo Farm.

By the end of 1930 Dad had remarried and I was back in the fold in time to move to Wakes Farm at Eversholt. The farmhouse was at the end of a long drive, so we were about two miles from the village school. My nine year old sister Stancy took me to and fro on the pillion of her bicycle and I remember we came a cropper one day near some road works and we both got our knees covered in melted tar.

Only a year elapsed before Dad had enough of trying to manage two farms, so far apart and we migrated back to Pertenhall, which was good news as far as I was concerned. However, the next problem was that I did not get on too well with my stepmother and I spent more and more time with my Grandparents back at Manor Farm.

Grandma was a big influence on me as I grew up and looking back not many women in their mid sixties would have the patience to start rearing a second brood. She was a very religious lady attending church services twice every Sunday and was of the firm opinion that God was the guiding light to all believers and before going to bed she read a short passage from the bible every night. She would visit any person in the village who was unwell taking them a small gift to suit, sometimes a homemade cake, half a dozen eggs, a basket of apples or a bunch of flowers.

Later in life I quite often went to see the widow of Grandfather's head stockman and she put me wise to happenings of long ago. The most unusual, an account of when her husband was stricken with rheumatic fever which would keep him laid up for a couple of months. At the end of the first week, Grandfather called to see how the patient was progressing and hearing that he would be off work for sometime, told the stockman's wife that she would have to pay half a crown rent per week as he would have to employ extra labour to cope with the work that the stockman did at weekends, which covered the rent for their tied cottage. The stockman's wife had to agree, but this would leave the family short of money for the rest of the week. Grandfather called on Saturday mornings for the rent and then Grandmother went round to the lady's house on Sunday evenings, after church and gave her the half crown back, on the understanding that she told no one about it. Society has come a long way since this happened, about seventy five years ago, but if we all

Manor Farm, Pertenhall, Claude's grandparent's home

have to tighten our belts nowadays, that will be no bad thing because most people spend money as if there is no tomorrow, where as we were taught to put a bit away for a rainy day.

When I was about ten years old Grandmother told me when I grew up she would give me my birth certificate which showed a different date than the one I was born. The reason for this discrepancy being in January 1926 there was a general strike of public sector workers, so the local office that registered birth and deaths was closed for quite some time. When it eventually opened my Father and one of his friends went to St. Neots in the buggy and according to her the state they were in arriving back home suggested that they had stopped for a drink at most of the pubs on the journey. Consequently when it came to giving the date for the Clerk to put on the Certificate neither of them could remember and took a chance on the 27th. So then not only did I have two homes, but two birthdays as well. Nowadays with so much form filling I have to remember on official documents to put the 27th but continue to celebrate my anniversary on the 25th. There can be no wonder at my time of life that my brain occasionally goes on the blink and the 25th gets on some official documents and recently my long suffering wife had a letter from the DHSS asking if there were two Mr. Banks residing at 20 Ashfield one born on the 25th and one on the 27th!

This is one of the occasions where the truth is stranger than fiction. Until now she has not been accused of bigamy nor have I been lucky enough to be granted two old age pensions.

I think that should be enough for the introduction except that any money made from the sale of these books will be divided between the Pertenhall and Kimbolton Churches in memory of Kate Banks my Grandmother. Without her love and kindness and guidance I would never have had the confidence I found myself with and her favourite motto, "If at first you don't succeed, try try and try again," is well worth remembering when things don't go according to plan.

College Farm

There is quite a bit of history attached to our small farm so I thought it would be helpful to describe how it has evolved during my lifetime.

I first came down to it as a four year old boy with my Grandfather in 1930. His main farm at that time was the 660 acre Manor Farm at Pertenhall and this 150 acres was all old ridge and furrow pastures. It comprised four 25 acre fields, one 40 and one 10, all surrounded by high hawthorn hedges, and over the years another 50 acres have been added. The only buildings on the farm at that time were a cattle yard with two open hovels and a loosebox where the grain store is now. The livestock Grandfather kept down here were store cattle, young horses and in foal mares and the field where the house is now was mown each year for hay and the stacks were built where the cherry tree is today.

Grandfather retired in 1937 and Dad took over the tenancy of the farm which belonged to one of the Colleges, as did most of the farms round here. Other farms belonged to the Church Commissioners. Come the war, we had to start ploughing it up and cutting down the hedges to increase production.

When I married in 1955, Dad had the house built for us and by then we had included sugar beet, potatoes and sprouts into our rotation. About this time Kimbolton airfield was being dismantled and by then we had our own lorry so we were able to construct a network of roads, using aggregate from the redundant runways, round the fields to access the root crops.

With the generous grants that were available later on we had the reservoir constructed in 1976 and for the next twenty years were able to produce good quality vegetables. But by the mid 1990's the

MANOR FARM,

PERTENHALL,

BEDS.

(5 miles from Kimbolton L.M.S. Station, 11 miles from Bedford, 8 miles from St. Neots).

IMPORTANT SALE OF

LIVE AND DEAD

Farming Stock

COMPRISING

20 Horses, 111 Cattle, 418 Sheep, 41 Pigs,

Agricultural Implements and Machinery for a 650-acre farm

AND

Surplus Household Furniture,

WHICH

Henry H. Bletsoe & Son

favoured with instructions from H. C. BANKS, Esq., will Sell by Auction upon the premises on

Friday, October 1st, 1937.

Sale to commence with the Implements at 11 o'clock prompt.

Light Refreshments will be obtainable.

For further particulars apply to the Auctioneers' Offices, Thrapston, Northants. (Tel. 4).

Scanned document Manor Farm Pertenhall

supermarkets had put paid to the small vegetable shop trade and by then I had reached 70 and decided to semi retire, move into the village. My daughter, Sally and her family came to live in the Farm House and we brought in contractors to do the farming.

This has worked quite well as I am able to turn up everyday and help to keep everything ship shape. I have been involved in our local farmers' shoot since it started in 1946 by Jim Cook who lived at Hoo Farm. When he passed away in 1970 the wild bird population had been fading away and we decided to plant the two spinneys in 1976, so that in time we had roosting space and somewhere to erect two release pens.

Somewhere around we have an old map of the farm which shows the ridge and furrows on the house field were owned by different people and the names of some of these appear on tombstones in Kimbolton Cemetery. There is still evidence, in some of the hedges that these were used as jumps for the Oakley Hunt Point-to-Point races which were held between 1880 –1908 and we have found copies of some of the race cards.

I well remember that first day's visit with Grandfather and how many blackbirds, thrushes and skylarks there were around, as collecting bird's eggs was something all boys did at that time.

Dad was able to buy the farm at the end of the war and now it has been passed on to Sally who like me is keen to help wildlife flourish with the reservoir and the two spinneys the key to success.

We have been informed that the piece of land the other side of the Pertenhall Brook was once a Roman settlement so a metal detector will have to be on my next shopping list.

CHAPTER ONE

Farming & Shooting

Have you any Wool

Our family has been in the farming business as far back as records show and with the large families that were produced it is no wonder that some members decided to emigrate. Delving back through the family tree, some went to Australia and others to Kenya and one on a trip to Canada that was well planned although kept secret.

Uncle Bert, one of eight children, turned out to be the black sheep of the family; he struck up a friendship with one of the blacksmith's sons who was also employed on the farm. This lad seemed to have the knack of getting into trouble and although christened William, he was always known as Gordon, because at that time it was popular to give boys around the age of ten years old the gift of a sailor's round hat, bearing the name of one of the battleships of the British Navy. One day the two boys had gone scrumping apples in the vicarage garden and were caught by the parson, who, seeing the name on the hat, said "Right Gordon, I will tell your father to give you a good hiding". That's how his name stuck.

I suppose it was Bert who was the ringleader, but one Saturday in the early 1900's, when they were about eighteen years old and knew that his father was not going to market that day, decided to take three fat bullocks from one of their fields bordering Swineshead village. They must have started out early to herd these bullocks to Bedford cattle market before sale time; afterwards they went to the office and said that Mr. Banks would like to be paid in cash which was not unusual. The two boys then went to collect new suits from Bert's father's tailor and a case of whisky from the wines and spirits merchant, they then took a train to Liverpool and set sail for Canada planning to go across to the Yukon for the gold rush.

However, I can only presume that with the women, wine and song, the money ran out before they reached their destination and the family sent money for Bert to sail back, but Gordon had to work his passage home as stoker on a steam ship.

A party was held at the farm on the return of the prodigal son and he was soon married and installed in a small farm in Bolnhurst. This lasted about two years then he went broke, then after another year back on the family farm he was put in a farm at Eltisley.

This was during the first world war and the winter had been as wet as ours this 2013/2014 and at breakfast one morning a knock on the door revealed a pair of well heeled briefcase carrying "nerds" explaining to Uncle Bert that they had come to inspect his farm to possibly use it as an airbase. True to form he had the last laugh when he explained that his land was so wet it would be more suitable as a submarine base.

He survived on his second farm about a year longer than his first farm, before going back home to recharge his batteries. Next stop was a farm in Norfolk in 1921, which turned out to be the drought year, the spring sown crops had not even germinated by harvest and this brought the end of his farming career.

That just about did it for Uncle Bert's farming career and he spent the next few years as a "Stop-me-and-buy-one" for Walls ice cream.

When I was a small boy with my grandparents, I was taken one evening by Grandpa down to "The Elms" where all the old aunts, some maiden, some widows resided. Grandad had a coffee; mine was cocoa but too hot to drink. After a time Grandad said "Come on boy your Grandma will wonder where we are". So I poured my cocoa into the saucer, blew on it and slurped it down. Later on I was told that Aunt Priscilla had said, "She had never seen such a badly behaved boy and the odds were that he would finish up worse than Uncle Bert".

That was one of the hurdles in life I think I cleared safely.

A Tale from the days when Shank's Pony was the Modus Operandi

This story relates events that happened less than one hundred years ago and seems as improbable as the moon landings.

It starts in the early 1920's when a small holding with a thatched cottage and a couple of ramshackle buildings came up for sale. It comprised three small fields totalling about fifteen acres that lay mid-way between Hoo Farm and Little Hoo Farm and only negotiable by a grass track. The reason for its position presumably was that it lay comfortably in a fold, in a contour of the land that protected it from the worst of the weather from the west, north and east but most of all a natural spring that provided all the year round drinking water. These were not the best credentials to attract a prospective buyer, but everything has its price and it is amazing to what lengths some will go to achieve independence. There was such a person, Mr. Henry Dickens from Bozeat who with money borrowed from the bank and accompanied by his daughter Anna, started life anew at "The Little Hoo Holding". How the economics could stack up to allow two people to live off and pay a mortgage on such a small property takes a bit of working out.

Anna had a boyfriend Joe Howe, who also lived at Bozeat and such was the strength of the bond between them that the twelve miles as the crow flies was nothing more than a minor inconvenience. For about six years Joe walked to Pertenhall after work on Friday evening and back on Monday morning to start his work on a farm in Bozeat at 7am. This lends substance to the theory that there is a commodity that "will draw men farther forward than gun powder will blow them back". Mr. Dickens died about 1928 and Joe was then able to move in with Anna and all went well until the summer of 1930 when the thatched cottage was destroyed by fire. A few days later Miss Kate Cook, who lived at Hoo Farm and was the infant teacher at Pertenhall School brought in several silver coins that were salvaged from the ashes which had become misshapen by the heat. We were all allowed to closely inspect them.

Luckily the neighbouring property, Little Hoo Farmhouse, was vacant at the time and the owners, the Duke of Manchester Estate, allowed Joe and Anna to rent the house. This arrangement suited all concerned as empty properties soon deteriorate, and of course in those days vandalism was unheard of.

The depression, we are now experiencing is but a flea bite compared with conditions at that time and the couple were in dire straights with increasing expenditure and virtually no income, but country people in those days would extend a helping hand to the needy. Anna negotiated a deal with Jim Cook the owner of Hoo Farm. He would take the small holding and pay off the mortgage and give them the market price for their two cows. In return they could live rent free for the rest of their lives in one of his empty cottages.

Anna died in 1950 and Joe very soon became almost a recluse, venturing out of the house only in the best weather. He was always dressed from head to foot in black and the old sack he wore around his shoulders was as black as his trousers. Once when I was filling up the drill on the Little Hoo Farm I had a feeling that I was being watched and sure enough in a gap in the hedge stood Joe, just staring, and I was glad to get back to the tractor and carry on with the work. He must have had a resilience and inner strength that propelled him to and fro from Bozeat in his younger days and with considerable help from the Reynolds family that lived next door he lasted until 1954 ending a story that is unlikely to be repeated and takes a lot of believing compared with life as it is today.

A Plague of Rabbits

The Kimbolton and Gt. Staughton estates dominated the shooting scene in this area between the two World Wars and probably for a long time before that. They both owned large wooded areas ideal for holding pheasants through the cold winter months, as well as considerable acreage of adjoining farm land. During the depression extra ground was hired from local farmers for the game shooting, particularly the English partridge that were abundant during that era and thrived on the mixed arable and pasture that suited their particular needs. They provided wonderful testing shooting during the early part of the season and a friendly rivalry existed between the two shoots as to which could provide the best days sport.

The size of the bag is a combination of the number of birds presented and the skill of the team of guns, with King George V often a guest at Kimbolton during the 1920's and considered as one of the best shots in the country. At that time the estate employed a head keeper and four under-keepers, each one responsible for a section of the shoot known as a 'beat', and had up to 100 traps each to set in tunnels for the small ground vermin, snares for the larger variety and to prove their efficiency a vermin pole to display their victims.

The rabbit population, renowned for its ability to reproduce, took full advantage of its chief predators the fox and stoat which had been virtually eliminated, had honeycombed the woods with their burrows which owing to the tree roots were impossible to ferret, and soon began to ruin all crops within half a mile of their warrens.

At the end of the shooting season a plan was hatched to try and solve the problem. Brown paper, coated with tar, was pushed down every hole and in a couple of days the rabbits were living above ground. The holes were then stopped up and a two day shoot produced a staggering bag of one thousand. This was well above expectation but their luck was beginning to run out.

The established custom was for the head keeper to meet the local game dealer at the "George Hotel" each Monday evening to discuss the likely total of game to be disposed of during the week and the dealer paying for the drinks. His price of 8d for shot rabbits did not appeal to the keeper as he had heard they were making 10d at Bedford auction, so he split the total and two men set off early Saturday morning with the farm wagon for the five hour return journey and put a 10d reserve on them.

Later in the day the estate office received a phone call saying they had not reached the reserve price and would they collect them first thing next morning. The two under-keepers were not amused at another half days extra work but orders were orders. The five hundred rabbits were allowed to stay on the wagon and off they went to St. Ives on Monday morning. Same reserve price, same result, not sold but during the proceedings twenty were pinched off the back of the wagon. Home again and unloaded into the game larder as the weather was warming up, and reloaded on Thursday and off to St. Neots. This time no reserve and they were sold for 8d less 10% commission.

The Kimbolton estate has always provided plenty of grist for the rumour mill and this was a costly mistake because everyone was a loser, especially the head keeper, who, from then on, had to pay for his own drinks at the George on Monday evenings and should have known that "A bird in the hand is worth two in the bush".

Life in the Slow Lane

Another shooting season is over and everyone is wondering where the time has gone. As we get older this is something we must learn to expect but the alternative is nothing to get excited about either. A far cry from school days when on occasion time seemed to go backwards, especially during the maths periods when the master rambled on about tangents, cosines and Pythagoras who invented theorems, seemingly designed to addle the brains of unsuspecting boys who could not wait to get out on the playing field with a ball.

My first visit to Kimbolton was in the Easter holidays in 1930 with my grandfather in his buggy. The old pony was tied to one of the hitching posts on the 'money side' of the street while Grandpa did the shopping and had a drink at the Lion Hotel. At that time for most people the horse was the modus operandi and although the railways had honeycombed the countryside getting passengers and goods to and from the stations was a problem solved by the trusty steeds.

Labour in those days was plentiful and cheap which was a good thing because a horse and cart could only carry one ton of grain or coal and needed a man to drive it along. Before the age of steam most freight was transported on barges along the rivers and canals, each one with a load of several tons pulled by a horse walking along the towpath and the driver more concerned whether he could afford another packet of Woodbines than the amount of methane gas the horse was producing or the negative value of its carbon footprint.

Those of our generation who are still kicking around are living in worrying times where most of the things we were taught to respect have disappeared down the plug hole. University educated politicians have replaced the Statesmen we trusted to guide us along life's straight and narrow path. Every few days there is another scandal with fingers in the till and broken promises, the list too long and depressing to complete.

We grumble about the forty ton Lorries that sometimes clog up our country lanes but they are far more efficient than 40 horses and carts. Cars too are getting bigger and were it not for the seatbelt law, some four-wheel drive vehicles could squeeze in a seven-a-side rugby team. Shades of the days when Henry Ford produced the Model T and you could have any colour you wanted, as long as it was black!

One of the advantages the horse has over the internal combustion engine is its ability to reproduce the species. No one has yet opened the garage door and found a new mini snuggled up beside their top of the range Land Cruiser. Wind the clock back to Coronation Day in May 1937, dad's best mare gave birth to a handsome colt foal but during labour she tragically died of a heart attack. Luckily we were able to hand rear the colt and in due course he was able to take his mother's place between the shafts and he lived happily ever after.

Blood and Tears

As February 2nd arrives with a deafening silence and the twelve bores cleaned for the last time, the shooting fraternity move towards the drawer marked "Sackcloth and Ashes" to begin their annual period of mourning. Our season has been a bit like the "Curate's Egg" only good in parts but the elders of the community have been well versed in what life was like during the pre-war depression, when it was accepted that half a loaf was better than no bread. Then, most farmers let their shooting, mainly English Partridge to the Duke of Manchester, the rent one shilling per acre.

Shooting, being a product of the farming industry, is not the cheap affair it was in those days when wild birds proliferated in the mixed farming and high hedges. Now with the landscape looking as bare as a baby's bottom, the movement of a field mouse could be picked up by a satellite just before it disappears into the undergrowth.

In 1976 we planted a couple of spinneys and are now reaping the benefit with warm roosting space and substantial release pens for our reared birds; until vandals turned up and smashed one of them to smithereens which left me in tears. Sometimes I wonder if it's all worth while. In days gone by these 'ner'-do-wells' would have been sent to Borstal. There used to be one such up Gaynes Hall in Perry and they had a football team in the Hunts League. We used to enjoy that fixture because we had a warm bath afterwards, unlike matches at The Park where we had sweet F.A. and had to bike home with mud caked knees.

One of the most enjoyable aspects of a farm shoot is the "Après Ski" (not a fling with the barmaid at the Local) but an evening meal at the farmhouse or pub followed by, if you are extremely lucky, a game of cards. During the time I was with my grandparents the card game was solo, but now with more money around it is Shoot Pontoon or Poker. This is good entertainment but don't get involved in Three Card Brag as you may lose more than just the housekeeping.

In the old days Grandfather's guests had to be content with a day's rabbiting which took place up the "Top Spinney", known in those days as "Ladycrafts", an oblong affair surrounding an acre or so of pasture. The windward side comprised of oaks and elms, spaced with hawthorns and on the lee side ash stools that were coppiced in rotation and the timbers used for making hurdles for stock proofing before wire netting was invented. A fire was lit in a sheltered spot and at lunch time a hamper packed by Grandma with all the goodies fit for a King, let alone we lesser mortals.

And so it was in December 1936. I was wearing my school mac because it was the only one I had and on the way back someone shot a hare, so yours truly grabbed it to carry home. The problem became apparent; because of my short legs the hare dragged along the ground so I slung it over my shoulder. When we got back to the farm, about a mile away, the hot water I got into had to be used first, to clean the fur and blood off the mac that Grandma had bought for me to start at KGS some three months earlier.

The Guns – Farm Shoot 1990

One Man Went to Sow

Early this spring time, I was busy repairing our cart roads when the contractors turned up to top dress a 25 acre wheat field with Nitram. The tractor seemed to be travelling at about ten miles an hour and spreading a width of 24 metres along tramlines already put in place by the drill, the job was done in not much more than half an hour. The hopper was topped up by a forklift raising half ton bags which were slit with a knife and are then no more use, just another example of the throwaway world we live in. How many acres the machine could cover in a day working on a thousand acre prairie is open to conjecture and a far cry from when our dad bought his first consignment of artificial fertiliser.

This was in about 1936 and the product, sulphate of ammonia, also a nitrogenous stimulant, a ton of which was delivered in hessian sacks which when emptied were used time and time again around the farm. Mid March and the target crop was a field of winter oats and the recommended dose one hundredweight (112 lbs) to the acre. Mechanical spreaders had not been invented at that time and Vic Roddis, a young guy who had just started working for us drew the short straw to broadcast it by hand. Fifteen of the bags were spaced out across the middle of the field and a bucket that held about a stone (14 lbs) for him to use. A couple of problems quickly became apparent. The fertiliser was brown in colour and impossible to see once it hit the ground, unlike Nitram Prills, that are white and easily visible. Secondly it was granular, similar to the sugar we put in our tea but very slippery to handle. The job took most of the day and we sat back and waited for the result, but like Christmas it was a long time coming and when it did Vic had enough egg on his face to last a life time.

After a warm spell and some April showers the field had taken on a zebra effect with dark green crescent shaped stripes where the stuff had landed and wider stripes of light green that had none and by harvest the dark green stripes were a foot taller than the rest, so it obviously did the job it was supposed to. The story does not end there because the five bags that were surplus were left on the dirt floor at the back of the cart hovel and by the next spring had set like rock, which provided a wet day job breaking it up. This happened so many times we lost patience and laid the solid mass out on the lane and gave it the treatment with a tractor and rim roll, loaded it on a trailer and spread it on one of the meadows.

I am not sure what the time and motion boffins would make of some of the things we got up to in those days but farms in this area were half arable and the rest pasture with livestock that provided work for most of the men in the villages. The rule of thumb would be one man for every fifty acres, now with the all arable regime and farm animals relegated to the endangered species list, the huge machines that roam the landscape mean that one man per five hundred acres is something of an expensive luxury.

New Territory to Explore

One Friday teatime in the spring of 1938, Dad announced that he had taken the tenancy of Little Hoo Farm. This was a property about 400 yards from the Moravian Chapel at Pertenhall, along a muddy track, which was almost overgrown with brambles.

Dad had gone down to Kimbolton that morning, Friday being the day that Barclays Bank from St. Neots was open for business. He was approached by Miss Carter the agent for the Manchester Estates. The conversation went something along these lines – "Good morning Charlie", "Good morning Miss Carter". "I would like to have a word with you". "How can I help?" "I wonder if you would like to take the Little Hoo Farm". "Take it where?" "Now don't be silly, you know what I mean". Dad – "I have enough problems trying to farm at the moment, without landing myself with another 70 acres of anthills, thistles and bushes!" Miss Carter – "I know it is not in very good shape but it would connect up to the land you farm at Stonely". "That is a good point, but not enough to tempt me". "Well, have it for a year, rent free and then if it is any good to you we will think about the rent to be paid".

Not wanting to look a gift horse in the mouth, Dad accepted the challenge, which suited me down to the ground, as, a few months before, Grandfather had retired from farming, I was feeling cramped up, having had his huge farm to roam over, for the previous seven years. The Hoo Farm had actually been without a tenant for some time, the previous people having done a moonlight flit owing a couple of year's rent, but they had left behind two sheep, which we christened 'The Ovaltinies', the nearest we could get to their previous owners, the Overtons, who had scarpered!

The farm buildings were pretty spartan, one loose box, one bay cart shed and two open cattle hovels, surrounded by a crew yard. The house was surprisingly in decent shape with a sound tiled roof. The walls were timbered mud and stud and the floors, brick onto the earth. A small scullery housed the inevitable copper, a must in every house however large or small in those days. The window looking south-east had a view further than Little Barford Power Station – a building site today, a view like that would be worth far more than the 72 acres of land. The kitchen had a cooking range with one window overlooking the garden, another window overlooking the cattle yard and a spacious 'front room', now-a-days known as the lounge. One large and two smaller bedrooms completed the building. If you think I have forgotten a toilet and bathroom, this is because they did not appear in many houses until after the War. Good quality water from a spring, fed a well, and a pump that worked provided one of the main requisites for survival.

The strangest thing about the set-up was the fact that there were two outside lavatories, one brick built in the south-east corner of the garden (they were never in the south-west corner) and one to the east, which was made of wood, but with a brick floor. Once the War got under way, country dwellings became greatly sought after and the house was then inhabited for the next 20 years. When the gale came on the night of 26th March, 1947, it blew the wooden lavatory clean over. I only hope it was not occupied at the time!

Chadwell Farm, Pertenhall, Claude's childhood home, with his bedroom window top right

Little Hoo Farm

Although the house was found to be in reasonable shape, the same could not be said about the land, which turned out to be, not much more than a huge rabbit warren. It had been severely under stocked since the 1921 slump and bushes and brambles covered large areas. The hedges had not been maintained and were up to 20 yards wide in places. So tackling the rabbit problem was going to be a headache. Fortunately Dad was friendly with a guy named Jessie James, who used to come for a walk round with his gun on the farm at Stonely. Mr. James got in touch with the Rushden Terrier Club, who, in the autumn, turned up with a pack of about two dozen assorted Jack Russells and mongrel dogs, so we all had a whale of a time on Sunday mornings, hunting out the hedges. I have no idea how many they killed, but they were allowed to keep 'the bag' and it must have been worth their while, as they kept up the good work for a long time.

After about six months, I think Dad decided that he could make something of the new land, as at least he could increase his sheep flock. At this time, Neville Chamberlain came back from Munich, waving a piece of paper saying 'Peace in our time', but it was obvious that war was not far away and it is still not a bad way of viewing most of the profound statements made by Prime Ministers.

Early in 1939, in response to the call to increase production, one eight acre field was tidied up, ploughed and prepared for drilling spring oats. That turned out to be the easy part, as when the seed should be emerging, we found that wireworms and leather jackets had eaten most of it. However our Smythe drill, with its Suffolk coulters was able to re-drill with barley, without disturbing those oats which had kept growing and the advice was to keep rolling the crop, to help it survive. That became my job, every Saturday, for about a month and as the roller was only eight feet wide; my initial excitement had plenty of time to revert to boredom, but 'ours not to reason why!' Basically farming, in those days, was more of a way of life, than a business.

The harvested crop was nothing very brilliant, but at least we were off to a flier, with the War getting under way in the autumn and we had another very much bigger field ploughed, up at Stonely. On Saturday mornings during the winter months, if we were not needed on the farm, myself and my younger brother, Bob, went rabbiting round the new land. Setting off on our bikes, with a couple of dogs, a spade and a number three garden gun, during one day, we bagged 26 rabbits, which is not bad going for a couple of boys, average age 11 years.

Most fields had at least one pond and there were several moats, which were quite deep and ideal for the moorhen population. Their eggs made a welcome addition to wartime rations. Dad was afraid that some small boys might drown whilst collecting these eggs, so he put a story around that there was a man-eating snake, which lived in the moat! One lad, who had become addicted to moorhen's eggs for breakfast, asked me if it was right that there was a snake-eating man living in the moat! Quite a giggle at the time, but 40 years later, he had the last laugh as yours truly, got a soaking, when the branch I was standing on snapped. I had been climbing a doddle ash, which every spring housed a mallard's nest, but luckily, that day, the 'man eating snake' was not at home!

Farming During the War – Part I

The low prices during the two decades prior to the start of WW11 had seen the agricultural industry plummet to unknown depths. Bankruptcy was rife, with many farmers turning to drink and even suicide, to try and escape the consequences. Owner-occupiers could not get out by selling their land, as no buyers were around, but one block of very heavy land was reputed to have changed hands for £5 per acre. Tenant farmers who could not pay their rent were not evicted, because prospective incumbents were conspicuous by their absence.

Many farmers adopted, what became known as, the 'dog and stick' method. The stick was the walking stick and the dog for rounding up the livestock. Some arable land was allowed to go back to nature and labour costs were severely reduced. Most banks had stopped lending the farmers any more money and it was left to the local corn merchants to give a helping hand by not invoicing for seed corn and livestock feed, but taking the harvested grain in settlement. In some cases, the farmer soon owed the merchant more than his farm was worth. The uncultivated arable land did not remain bare for long, as the birds distributed the seeds of blackberry and hawthorn, which with thistles and ant hills, colonised huge areas. If the War had not come along, the land would have become an impenetrable jungle, inhabited only by vermin and predators. By 1938, the Government which had perfected the art of doing nothing, gradually woke up to the fact that Hitler meant business and given the chance, would pose a threat to our food supplies, which were now coming from far off lands. To encourage farmers to increase production, a grant of £2 per acre was announced for voluntary ploughing up of grassland. This did not bring about the anticipated result and with the War now underway and the U-boats causing havoc in the shipping lanes, 'ploughing up' became compulsory and to ensure that it was carried out, the 'War Agricultural Executive Committee' was formed and became known as the 'War Ag' for short! This comprised a few of the better farmers, who had managed to keep their heads above water and some who had 'gone under', but had the time to go round and chivvy others, to get their act together. Those farmers, who could not or would not, had their land dispossessed and the War Ag then farmed it.

The big problem with ploughed up grassland was, creating a seedbed with traditional implements and it quickly became obvious that disc harrows were the only answer, but they were few and far between. The War Ag soon had a good labour force and implements for them to use and for hire to local farmers, but as we all know, everyone wants the same piece of kit at the same time. One local farmer, who had ploughed up a big field, at the top end of his property and had waited a long time for the discs to arrive, had to watch the War Ag in the adjoining field, making a nice seedbed, with a crawler tractor and set of discs. Sunday morning saw the tackle standing idle and he took his small wheel tractor and 'borrowed' the discs to work his field. 'Sods law' then came into play, where, in a wet patch, the discs became bogged down. Next morning, at the crack of dawn, with plenty of egg on his face and a five-pound note in his hand, he was standing by the crawler, waiting for the driver to turn up and get him out of trouble and, keep quiet about it!

There are old sayings to cover most eventualities and 'Be sure, your sins will find you out' fits this one quite nicely!

Farming During the War – Part II

There were plenty of initiatives available to help rejuvenate the farming industry, some of which were not much more use than giving a terminally ill patient a couple of aspirins! Money was the commodity most urgently needed, but the price of staple products like eggs, milk, meat, potatoes, wheat and feed grain, were controlled to stop racketeering. An open market was available for malting barley and the harvest of 1942 saw it exceed £80 per ton, which was more than four times the price of feed barley. The short supply was the result of pressure to grow wheat for bread making.

"Necessity is the mother of all invention," encouraged the maltsters to use almost any grain that would germinate, even if the resulting brew was not up to the highest standards. Weak beer was better than none at all! Some pubs often had 'sold out' notices on their doors and others rationed customers to one pint each. This could well have been where the saying 'the survival of the fittest' originated and lifted the undignified term 'pub crawl' to almost Olympic status!

An advisory service was set up by the Ministry of Agriculture and the chap allocated to North Beds was most helpful. The farming scene was going through rapidly changing times and, what to grow on the newly ploughed up grassland, was a major headache, with wire worms and leather jackets, two of the worst pests, which could devastate a crop in a few days, resulting in re-drilling which was time consuming and expensive.

Later on, a new crop was introduced called flax, which is a close relative of linseed, but is grown for its fibre. Special drills were needed, with closely spaced coulters, so that the growing crop competed and grew tall, to reach the sunlight. This crop was immune to the soil borne pests, which harmed the cereal crops, but the flip side was that it needed a special machine to harvest it, one that pulled, rather than cut the crop. Contractors carried out this operation, with the tractor driver out to break all land speed records, however rough the going and the machine operator, usually a land army girl, clinging to the seat, like a rodeo rider at the Calgary Stampede!

Draining the land was essential and grants were available to remedy this problem. The water logging over the years had made the soil very acid and several tons of lime per acre was needed to be applied, to enable the crops to flourish. One of the most useful farming implements ever made, became available in the autumn of 1941, imported from America and became known as the Combine Disc Drill. Separate compartments enabled the seed and fertiliser to be sown together and cut into the seedbed with disc coulters which increased yields immediately by as much as 50 %.

Cheap Italian prisoner-of-war labour became available at this time and they were pretty decent chaps, no more wanting the war than we did. Language was a problem early on, but they soon cottoned on to all the swear words! Some used to try it on by saying 'me no understand', when given a job they disliked, but would eventually condescend to do it. These altercations usually ended by the prisoner saying 'Bar Fungule', which I took to mean OK or alright. However, just recently, in Bedford, I was in conversation with an Italian, who emigrated here after the War, to work in the brickyards and he was interested in listening to the stories of his compatriots, working on the farms, during the War. This was my chance to have the meaning of the words 'Bar Fungule' explained, but I soon found out that this was a stone I should have left unturned, as translated it was the classic dismissal 'you can f... off'! Still, we can't win them all, can we?

Another Trip Down Memory Lane

Wartime conditions helped to accelerate the change from horsepower to the internal combustion engine and transformed farming activities, taking much of the drudgery away with it. The first tractors did not have rubber tyres and were two-wheel drive. This led to some of the old horse keepers, probably fearful of losing their jobs if tractors took over completely, forecasting that the land would suffer and crop yields diminish. Crawler tractors soon followed and did not compact the land to the same extent and further progress has seen massive four-wheel drive machines working round the clock, when conditions are favourable.

The previous century was dominated by steam power, not only in the railways and shipping industries, but also in agriculture. These engines were mainly contractor owned and travelled from farm to farm, as and when required and were in two categories. The cultivators, as they were known, each weighing up to twenty tons, worked as a pair, one at each end of the field and the implement, either a plough or scuffle, was hauled across by a steel cable, housed in a revolving drum, midway under the belly of the engine. A steam whistle was used as a method of communication and on still days, it was possible to know what was happening a couple of miles away. This was seasonal work, usually starting at the end of May, when the fallow land was given its first cultivation, then moving onto other fields, after crops were harvested. When the weather deteriorated, in late autumn, these machines were packed away until the following spring, but were usually only given the heaviest clay and the steepest slope to cultivate, which produced one of the old sayings, "that hard work may not have killed anyone, but it wore plenty of steam engines out". These machines had an appetite for coal and water, which seemed never ending and provision was the responsibility of the farmer. The latter was cheap enough, as long as the supply was not far away and the former not that expensive and was collected from the merchant at Kimbolton Station, in one ton cart loads, with some of the lumps weighing up to half a hundredweight (25 kilos) and tipped up in heaps around the field to be cultivated, for them to help themselves as and when required.

The gang comprised four men, one for each engine, one to operate the implement being hauled to and fro and one acting as cook and relief for any of the others needing a break. Part of this entourage was a caravan, for sleeping accommodation, the men only going home at weekends.

The second category of machine, was the threshing engine, which hauled the drum, elevator and chaff cutter round the villages and one never ceased to be amazed at the skill of the driver of these leviathan monsters that expelled smoke and steam in equal measure from every aperture. Some farm gateways were not that wide and the manoeuvring complicated, but they got there in the end, often accompanied by various adjectives and adverbs, which certainly helped broaden the vocabulary of anyone surveying the scene. The power from the engine was transmitted to the drum, by a flywheel and endless belt, with sundry pulleys and chains completing the cycle that saw the sheaves of corn fed into the top and grain, chaff and straw exiting, to be stacked and packed away in time honoured fashion. As well as the two operatives of the outfit, another half a dozen men, at least, were required for various tasks and all this took place in an atmosphere of choking dust, which had to be experienced to be believed. Health and Safety officials would have had the time of their lives and the fact that so few accidents happened, was as a result of concentrated and alert minds.

Small boys were attracted to these operations, in and out of school hours, to kill the rats and mice that had set up home in the corn stacks. It was not unknown for a young mouse to find its way into the school mistress's wellingtons, but two strokes of the cane on the backside of the culprit was deterrent enough to avoid a

Claude and Brother Bob, with dogs and Baler 1947

second helping. This type of punishment in now against the law and we are left with 'spare the rod, spoil the child', as a reminder that if the threat of the cane has to be removed, why are we spending billions of pounds on the Trident Missile. The Bible quotes that 'God moves in mysterious ways' – he may well have caught that complaint from Homo sapiens.

A Wolf at the Door

A recent television programme, featuring the National Park at Yellowstone in the USA, was most interesting, especially the wolf pack, which was still surviving, as much as it did a few centuries ago. They live entirely on meat and target the vulnerable in the grazing herds. Years later, the invention of the gun and bullet enabled these packs to be brought under control, so that farm animals could survive to feed an ever expanding population.

There are quite a few examples in folklore of the impact these beasts had on society, with the fate of Little Red Riding Hood's grandmother being the most striking. When we were at primary school the game known as 'Are you there Mr. Wolf' kept us amused and out of mischief. Everyone could take part, although the girls seemed to prefer skipping, especially with the long rope. Two of the older girls would do the turning, with half a dozen others taking part in a kind of continual motion process, with the one at the front hopping out and running round and joining in at the back, whilst the others all moved up a notch – a very effective keep-fit exercise.

During the depression, most families were being hard pressed and those who had experienced a particular run of bad luck were said to expect 'a wolf at the door', but all this changed when the War started and the economy picked up. Extra land had to be brought into cultivation, most of which was waterlogged by the neglect of ditches and brooks. The War Ag was soon underway, with drainage officer's available to help out with the planning. The chap allocated to North Beds, was, by one of those strange coincidences that crop up from time to time, named Mr. Wolf, so a knock on the door from him was good news, rather than bad. He and my Dad got on well together, as they both enjoyed a drop of the hard stuff and most visits usually included not only inspecting the field to be drained, but the inside of the Lion or the George in Kimbolton!

Ours should have been the best drained farm in the County, but at that time all the aggregate being produced had to go for building the airfields, so bushes had to be laid on the drainage pipes instead of gravel. After about 20 years, not surprisingly, the bushes had rotted away and consequently some of the fields needed to be re-drained. The War Ag did the contracting in the first instance and the machine cutting the trench could well have been produced by Dante before his blue print for The Inferno! Basically it was a Standard Fordson Tractor, with a reduction gearbox and fitted with tracks that clumped their way along at snails pace, whilst emitting enough black smoke to kick start the global warming process! This machine was called a 'Buckeye', which suggests it may have come over from the USA, but the placid nature of Ebenezer, the driver, lent an air of calm on an otherwise frantic operation. His philosophy was that anything done in a hurry has unforeseen consequences, with

Brother Bob on tractor and Claude, with Baler 1947

illegitimate children the by-product of certain activities that are carried out in too much of a rush! I am not sure if his knowledge of this statistic was first or second hand, but what is without doubt, 'there is many a true word spoken in jest'!

A Rather Expensive Bird

Rationing during the war did not stop until several years later and meat, always being expensive, meant that the price of game was up in the luxury bracket.

Poaching became a lucrative pastime, with one such miscreant often bragging that his nocturnal exploits were earning him more than his weekly wage at the RAE.

The keepers on the local estates were not too pleased to be wandering round their woods when the church clock was striking the midnight hour and everyone else in the land of nod. The Great Staughton keepers were more disadvantaged than the Kimbolton ones as several of their woods bordered the public highways, especially when a new type of poaching became popular. The Sunday morning mobile boys, two guys riding round in a car with one shooting out of the window and bagging several brace before the pubs opened at twelve o'clock. The price of petrol at that time, the equivalent of 10p per litre, now would be about £1.40 per litre, and pheasants in the feather about £2 per brace then and now 90p.

Something had to be done, so the two sets of keepers, together with several police, deployed in hiding round the vulnerable area one Sunday morning and lay in wait for the sound of gunshot. When it happened, the ones in the lay-by next to Stonely brickyard were first on the scene but instead of a couple of tearaway townies it was a local farmer coming out of his own field, gun under one arm and a cock pheasant in his other hand.

So what was the problem? The law of the land states that although you may shoot a wild duck on a Sunday but not a pheasant or partridge, and since the police were involved and being paid overtime the Chief Constable decreed that he be summoned to appear at the local assizes and was duly fined, no doubt "pour décourager les autres".

The ironic thing about this episode is that he was a quite inoffensive person and more a hunting man than a shooting one and most farmers, myself included, could say "There but for the grace of God go I". But at the end of the day he had broken the eleventh commandment. "Thou shall not be found out".

Just One for the Pot

After the war one of the forms of entertainment for some of us was going to football internationals up the smoke, once at Tottenham where England lost 2-0 to Italy. Our two most reliable chauffeurs were Billy Hall and Colin Robinson and in one particular match at Wembley about 1948 we were playing Scotland with Frank Swift our goalkeeper and Billy Houliston the opposing centre forward. After one attack Swift fielded the ball and cleared it but as he returned to his goal Billy Houliston brought his knee up into Frank's groin which floored him but with the play having moved up field neither the ref or linesman had spotted the foul, but he needed treatment by the medical staff.

The story now moves on about 25 years and weekend shooting trips organised by Oscar Jordan had become popular. On this occasion two car loads including Brian and Maurice Whitlock, Oscar, Claude Darlow, Colin, Bert Bates, (brother) Bob and myself set off for a weekend wildfowling up at Dumfries in Scotland and were booked in at a guest house named "The Nith".

When we arrived we decided to inspect the bar where an odd character with red hair and a beard to match was perched on a stool. It turned out he was a hotel keeper from York and after having a row with his wife decided a weekend away might clear the air, although by the look in his eye he seemed like a bloke that had lost a half crown and found a shilling but after a couple of days in our company the pendulum had swung so far he looked as if he had come across the half crown as well.

Most readers by now will have cottoned on to the fact that Billy Houliston and his wife were our hosts and they certainly turned on the style to make us feel welcome. Drinking and card playing took up about the same amount of time as skulking in a creek up to our knees in mud and seaweed, waiting in vain for a skein of geese to appear out of the gloom, and in one session I had enough Dutch courage to ask Billy why he did that nasty deed to Frank. He explained that just before, when one of their corner kicks came over, he went up to head the ball, but Frank came out to punch it clear and his fist connected with Billy's head, so retribution had to follow.

One night we were so late finishing cards and made so much noise going to bed that Bert and Colin, who were new kids on the block, had gone to roost early and started to get dressed thinking it was time to get up.

The upshot of the weekend was just one wild goose in the bag, shot by Brian, so his long suffering wife Dorothy had the job of preparing a slap up meal the next Saturday evening with the unfortunate bird and a large joint of pork for the eight protagonists and another session of cards.

On another occasion four of us set off well before dawn for a day wildfowling on the Holbeach marshes. There was a stinging frost and half way there the car conked out, the reason the carburettor had frozen up, so we had to take turns in standing on the upturned bonnet and directing a stream of pee onto the target area.

The fact that it did the trick endorsed the old saying that necessity is the Mother of invention.

Tea in the Harvest Field

Thermos flasks had not been invented when I was a boy and the favourite drink for farm workers, in the field, was bottles of cold tea, without milk or sugar. This does not sound very exciting, but it is the most thirst quenching of all and more importantly at that time was quite cheap. The main snag with flasks is that they often come to grief, as was the case when a lorry ran out of road on the Wellingborough bypass. The driver had to walk to the nearest phone box to ring his boss. "This is Bill, hive had a haccident". "Any damage?" "Hive broke me flask". It turned out that the lorry, laden with tarmac for the M1, had finished up in a ditch and was a write off!

During the 1950's we grew a field of tares. These are a vetch, not unlike maple peas and need swathing to ripen before combining. One of our neighbouring farmers did contract work and sent his swather, driven by an ex German POW, to cut the crop. When Dad went to see how he was getting on, the driver told him he had dropped his docky bag and broken his two flasks. Dad took him a jug of tea at lunchtime and when he had finished the job gave him ten bob for a tip and another ten bob for his broken flasks. Some time later the contractor got in touch and said he was sending his bill, plus an extra ten shillings, his worker had claimed for the two broken flasks! Not surprisingly, Dad was not amused and told the contractor that he had already paid for the b…y flasks once, and did not intend making another contribution! No wonder we are being short-changed by the EEC!

Many years ago, a farming couple's marriage was going through a difficult time. The wife was not a country girl and it was not until the children had fledged the nest, that she realised there were other opportunities to enjoy life, rather than rusting away on a lodge farm, with a husband who showed more interest in the farm, than to her. She had found a suitable alternative and was biding her time, before 'pulling the trigger'.

The moment came, during a harvest, where the weather was as bad as a summer we have recently experienced. At these times, every chance has to be grabbed, to get in a few more loads, before the monsoon rains return. Saturday morning arrived, with rain still leaking from leaden skies, the farmer promised the long-suffering wife, a bar snack that evening, at the local hostelry. Eros was not on his side. As soon as the words had left his mouth, the rain stopped, the wind got up and the sun came out. After lunch he was off on his combine harvester and Plan A – the bar snack, had gone right out the window. The good lady, game to the last, took his packed tea up the field and as he clambered down from his machine, she said "I am leaving you now". "Will you wait until I have finished my tea, so you can take the basket back, otherwise the flask might get broken."

An unsentimental parting, if ever there was one and perhaps Young Farmers advertising brochures should carry the warning, that marrying a farmer may seriously jeopardise your leisure time!

Surprise Surprise

On February 2nd when members of the game shooting fraternity were moving towards the drawer marked "Sackcloth and ashes", to begin a period of mourning, a rash of common sense broke out. Firstly the County Council vetoed the application for a wind farm on the old airfield site, and secondly it was announced that the panel of experts who had been cobbled together to prove that climate change was man-made and not the natural progressions we were taught by our Geography Masters at school, had been massaging the figures to come up with the required conclusions.

This comes as no surprise to the general public, whose opinion of politicians must be at the lowest ebb ever and should scupper their plans for a carbon emissions tax. They will then have to dream up new ways of raising finance and could do worse than follow the example of long ago when the then chancellor introduced a tax known as Morton's Fork. Those who spent lavishly were heavily taxed as they could obviously afford it, and those that spent very little were taxed even more because; they must have plenty saved up.

George Osborne could impose a tax on sex using Morton's formula in which case the Blairs would be hardest hit, because by Cherie's own admission, she spent most of her nocturnal hours at No.10 gazing at patterns on the bedroom ceiling.

The Beaters – Farm Shoot 1990.
Claude centre front between two small boys

To use up the remaining space allotted and carrying on roughly the same theme, a builder found himself the beneficiary of a substantial legacy and bought a semi derelict castle in Ireland with the proceeds. After carrying out the necessary repairs he went to live there and threw a few parties in celebration. The local police were suspicious of all this and decided to carry out a search which resulted in finding an illicit still behind a bricked up doorway in one of the cellars. Although completely innocent he was convicted at the trial for being the owner of the offending piece of equipment.

The judge in his summing-up, asked the defendant, as is usual in such cases, if he had any other criminal offences to be taken in consideration, the builder replied admitting to a case of rape. The judge thinking a can of worms was about to be opened up inquired of the date the offence took place, and the builder replied "It hasn't happened yet but I have the necessary equipment to carry it out".

Spoil Sports

The old saying that a dog is man's best friend is true as far as I am concerned, but my luck with the furry variety ran out many years ago.

When we married in 1955 our first dog was a Jack Russell which was ideal for when strangers turned up, he soon let them know they were not welcome. He was very good with our three children as they grew up and dealt with any rats that sought to take up home in the farm buildings. He also liked to join in when we went round shooting a few rabbits, but one trigger happy person obviously mistook him for the target and killed him stone dead. You can imagine how the children felt when they heard the bad news.

Daphne made the decision for our next four legged friend and later on a young Golden Labrador pup joined the family. We named him Rex and Daphne taught him to retrieve by hiding a stuffed sock with pheasant tail feathers sticking out round the garden.

When the shooting season arrived I took him over to Tilbrook where Roger and Eileen Dunkly were running the White Horse Pub, and he had permission to shoot over Harry Sansome's land. Rex was soon able to put his training into good use and over the next few years his exploits became legendary among the shooting fraternity.

At that time anyone with a Land Rover was a recipient for shooting invites, but with Rex, my phone kept ringing and once at Hail Weston he swam through the flooded River Kym and retrieved a strong runner that had fallen on the other side. Jack Pigg, whose farm we were on, said it was the best he had ever seen.

The fact that Rex's ability to find game, through following the scent trail, ultimately lead to his demise. He could always tell when a bitch was coming into season and we would get a call from either Jim Cook or Lionel Sapsed our neighbouring farmers to come and collect him.

Our daughter Penny had the job of going to fetch him back but

Mrs Cook was most off hand and whereas most farmers' wives would give a child a jam tart or a few sweets she gave her a ticking off as if it was all her fault.

Unfortunately the dog's love of the ladies resulted in his demise as on one his trips he disappeared and no one was able to help. He must have come to grief somewhere because had he been stolen, he was such a one-man-dog, I know he would have found a way back home somehow.

Not to end the story on a sad note, one of Rex's crowning glories was a day we were all invited to a shoot around the Kimbolton Airfield. The main drive was a large block of sugar beet with the guns and beaters walking the birds up. Rex the only dog on duty ranged in front of the line putting the birds up and retrieving them back to me after they had been shot. I think the bag on that drive was just under thirty and would have made a good film if video cameras had been around at that time.

Later on a drive was to take place through an area of scrub where concrete hard standing had been left and ideal for holding game. As we set off to beat through to the waiting guns we found a car with a couple engaged in what might better be described as nocturnal activity. The fact that they had decided to strip out and misted up the windows prompted our host to tap on roof and say "Warm work isn't it governor".

Whatever Next

The recent news that our last local pig farmer is preparing to throw in the towel brings more than a touch of sadness. That branch of the industry has always been a roller coaster affair with boom and bust close companions, and the fact that Neil is calling it a day comes as no surprise. He has been involved ever since he was knee high to a grass hopper and for many years supplying our local butcher with a product that is second to none. The secret is that he mills and mixes his own cereals adding molasses and various spices that give a unique flavour. All this comes at a cost that cannot be passed on to the customer who will turn to the supermarkets cheaper product.

When I was a boy Dad kept about half a dozen sows and fattened their offspring that were sold at St. Neots market. One of my jobs on a Saturday morning would be to walk one of the sows that had been weaned to visit the boar. Sometimes it would be to Mansfields Farm at Swineshead which was not too bad, about one and a half miles which was a snip compared with the other venue. That was on Uncle Harry's West End Farm, Little Staughton and although a short cut up Scotch Street, a green lane that shortened the journey, the round trip would be nearer five miles than four. The sow would be left with the boar in the honeymoon suite and I would run back home, quite what any eight or nine year old boy would make out of doing that job today could provide ammunition for another story.

We all wish Neil good luck as he takes a well earned rest from the daily chore and hope he can make a few bob out of selling his cereal crops instead of feeding them. That side of the industry has benefited by the rising prices owing to floods, drought and increasing population numbers, but the pendulum will swing back at some stage as sure as eggs are eggs because only a few years ago we had 10% compulsory set-a-side.

Life was never meant to be too simple but to wake up on a sunny spring morning and everything in the garden looking lovely; turning on the telly to find out Ireland beat us at cricket. Nothing should surprise us any more.

CHAPTER TWO

Cricket

Cricket: The Early Days

Our generation was lucky, in as much as we had no option but to make our own amusement and find ways and means to occupy our spare time. For a start everyone from about five years of age had jobs to do about the house or on a local farm. Cricket was one of the games used to fill in time between other activities. We played in the meadow, when the grass was dry and on the road at other times, with a couple of tin cans serving as wickets. One Saturday morning in the summer of 1934 five of us set off to play Lt.Staughton boys, two of us running, whilst the oldest boy took one in the basket and one on the pillion of his father's tradesman's bike. He dropped them off at the bottom of Spring Hill, came back and collected us and we all got up to the field together.

There was eight of the opposition, so they gave us one and the spare boy became known as a "Jackabo", who batted for both teams. There were no umpires or scorers, the batsman keeping count of his runs and everyone else fielding. The bumpy pitch meant that no one lasted long and we had several innings each and had plenty of energy left for the two and half mile trek back home. In the afternoon, the Keysoe boys came to Pertenhall with a team of six, three of which were Stapletons and all on foot. They were a large family, with one girl and eight boys, three of whom joined Pertenhall men's cricket team after the war.

So much emphasis now on football leaves me wondering why we never played that game and several valid reasons have surfaced. One reason could have been that Grandma Banks, who sponsored us with the bats, balls and wickets might have been reluctant to provide a football, which would have resulted in us wearing out our shoes and becoming unpopular with the other mothers. Another reason was that during the long winter months there were plenty of jobs for boys in grandfather's farm buildings. Sixty or more head of cattle were housed in several straw yards and their first feed of the day was known as "short grub", a mixture of chaff, sliced mangolds and either rolled oats or cattle cake and prepared one day ahead. The boys' jobs were topping and tailing the mangolds and putting them in the hopper of the "wezzle grinder", with a second boy furiously turning the handle. The cattle cake was one of the few commodities that had to be imported. Linseed cake from Canada and cotton cake from Egypt, the seeds crushed for their oil and the residue compressed into slabs about an inch thick, fifteen inches wide and a yard long. Each slab weighed about 10lbs and a 'boy powered' cake breaker chimbled it up into walnut sized lumps to provide the protein.

There were plenty of opportunities to get into mischief, but if boundaries were crossed, suitable punishment was exacted. No one enjoys pain, which is probably why visits to the dentist are the bottom of the popularity poll. The older brother of one of our little gang went a bridge too far, when he stole money from his grandparent's home. There was no family cover-up and the court ordered three strokes of the birch. That made a man of him and he was never in trouble again. He served five years in the army during the war and came back to enjoy a successful marriage and worked for the same firm until retirement.

Even if the old saying, "Believe nothing you hear and only half of what you see", were true, it is obvious in some areas, the law of the jungle has taken over and the authorities should wake up to that fact and deliver punishments to fit the crime.

Cricket – Part II

During my years at Lt.Staughton, the playing strength had increased to the stage where some youngsters were unable to get a game and with Pertenhall short of men I decided it would make sense to play for my home team. Success soon came our way and although initially we had only 12 players to select from we gained promotion in the Beds League from Division 3 through to the Premier Division in four years. Charlie Weller did a great job, tending our small square and the farmer Tom Bates was very supportive doing more than just hand out the awards at Club Dinners.

Tea was organised at Aunt Nell's cottage with plenty of volunteers to help out, which underlined her popularity. Nelly Banks was a staunch member of the Moravian community and indeed was one of the last people to be laid to rest in the Moravian grave-yard at Chapel Yard.

We are all aware that distance lends enchantment, so it is not surprising that most of the interesting stories relate from pre-war days, when Sid Shelton regularly scored more than half the runs and Alf Pedley was the demon spin bowler. Although time is regarded as a great healer it also eroded ability and eventually Alf's bowling became so expensive he was dropped for the match at Hargrave, but he was a cussed old chap and everyone chickened out of telling him. Consequently 12 men took to the field and when the captain did pluck up the courage Alf promptly sat down in the middle of the pitch and true to form refused to budge, so one of the others had to act as twelfth-man.

Visits to the archive unearth a mass of facts and figures, but there is no substitute for that which comes straight from the horse's mouth, so I went along to see Bernie Ashpole the only survivor of an extraordinary match played at Pertenhall in 1939. It took place in continuous rain with the home team all out for 13 and when the opponents, Wilden, were seven down for seven runs the game was called off as a draw, with both teams afraid that they were going to lose and we all retired to the barn, where the mower was stored and a sing-song took place. "We're gonna hang out the washing on the Siegfried Line", was one song which was repeated over and over, along with many others. Little did we know that within a few months four of the Pertenhall team would go off to War, only for two of them to return.

According to Bernie, Pertenhall was the favourite venue for visiting teams because of the quality of Granny Roddis' teas. She had produced and reared eight children and certainly needed no further instructions to overcome the age old problem of sucking eggs, because amongst the fare on offer was home-made Swiss-roll preceded by squares of cold yorkshire pudding with jam on it!!

Modern players would not rave over these sorts of teas, but at that time we were just coming out of a recession that had lasted eighteen years and everyone had learnt to live within their means, which is probably more than can be said today.

The Wizard of Dean

Over the last century there has been a spectacular change in village life. At the turn of the last century, probably 90 per cent of the population was reliant on agriculture and this has now dropped to less than 10 per cent. The village of Dean is a typical example, where, in the early days, most of the land was owned by two families and the present population is lucky, in as much that both families channelled a considerable amount of largess for the benefit of future generations.

Colonel and Eileen Wade lived at The Grange and owned the farm, as well as numerous cottages housing employees whom were well supported in times of stress. Mrs Wade's father, William Ackroyd, provided funds in 1863 for the United Chapel to be built, so it is no wonder the villagers looked no further than her name for the new primary school.

The Daltons owned most of the land at the other end of the village and were equally supportive, bequeathing funds to provide a community hall and playing fields, as well as a lump sum invested for an annual Christmas hamper for OAP's and a Children's party. Three pubs gave the locals plenty of choice, but The Three Compasses, the only one to survive, was once kept by Harry Hewitt whose day job was groom and chauffeur to Col.Wade. He so impressed his boss at solving any problems the Col said that he must be a wizard, a nickname that stuck and made Harry justly proud.

Years ago in most villages, one family outnumbered all the others and at Dean it was the Harts, when at one time they numbered 18 and now, like in the Agatha Christie story – "now there are none."

The cricket team was always a force to be reckoned with especially during the thirty years Vic Horsford was captain. He was a stubborn opener and often carried his bat through the innings. Now it is most encouraging to see the present day Club forging ahead and supporting the boys' teams, of all age groups, playing in league cricket. There must be many hands at the pump to have come this far because there is no substitute for hard work and when looking to succeed, especially today, when many Clubs have thrown in the towel.

Harvey Lilley was the butcher at Lower Dean after being de-mobbed until retirement and was at Kimbolton Grammar School one year ahead of our intake. He took me home for tea on a couple of occasions, when Dean had a home match in the John White Knock-out Cup and they sometimes used guest players to strengthen their line-up, with Harry Davison, Ollie and Stan Stapleton often taking part. I recall Stan's 92 year young widow, Lizzy, telling me that she and Stan would cycle the six miles from Thurleigh after leaving work at 5 o'clock, change, no time for tea, play the game and bike back. No need for fitness classes in those days.

My first recollection of Dean, was going there with a boys' team in 1935 when we were on the end of a good hiding and the gruelling ride back, up the hills, through Swineshead, I shall never forget. Thirty years later I was shown a cricket score book that contained details of that match and one of our batsman was listed as:-

SEABANKS Bowled K.Hart 9

Mind you, I have been called worse names than that since then!

More from the Playing Fields

After WWII had ended there were opportunities to play for invitation XI's as well as for the regular club teams. The Beds NFU Secretary was very sport minded and arranged games with various opponents including the Insurance company at Stratford-on Avon, both at football and cricket, using the facilities at Potton as our home ground. The cricket captain was Dick Sanders, a wealthy farmer from out Turvey way, the typical hunting, shooting and cricketing type who actually had his own cricket pitch at Snelson.

Dick set up games versus the local (fox) Hunts and arranged fixtures with the Carlton School of handicapped boys. Those games were memorable for the way these youths, although afflicted in body or mind, put so much effort into their play, some were brilliant fielders and one in particular could run faster than the proverbial hare and never dropped a catch. They were very sobering occasions and I have often thought how lucky those of us are, to be reasonably "compos mentis" and able to enjoy life with work, sport and family, that we should never need grumble again.

Towards the end of summer 1945 I was able to achieve a life long ambition seeing a day's play in a test match at Lords. England v the Australian Service Men. We cycled to Bedford and with a return ticket to St. Pancras, tube to St. Johns Wood, to see a day's play, food and drink as necessary and arrive home with a little change out of a £1 note.

Sunday cricket soon appeared on the scene much to the annoyance of some of the older generation, but the war had broken up customs as well as societies and we were just as Christian on the field as we would have been in church, so when an opportunity came to play on Sundays for the Igranic Works team at Bedford this was a step in the right direction. They had superb facilities and all matches seemed to be played at home.

During the summer of 1952 I was one of an invitation team to play on a Sunday against Ramsey and although the match finished up as a tame draw I had a decent knock. This was the turning point in luring me away from village cricket. The next season I joined Kimbolton where I soon found that everything in the garden was far from lovely. Most of the team that had won the Smith Barry Cup in 1947 had retired or left to join other clubs and having had many successful seasons in the past, extra effort would be needed to lift the club from the doldrums. However, in 1957 Jeff Hart from Dean joined and before long we were on an upward curve but it was not until 1959 tangible success came our way in the shape of the Bedford Hospital Cup. That was a very popular competition in those days and well over a hundred clubs taking part with the first round taking place before the end of April when we played Colworth House at Sharnbrook. The unusual aspect of the game was owing to a late start and time spent looking for lost balls. The match ended long after sunset and as we came off the field our footprints showed up in the grass that was covered in the rime frost. Definitely a two sweater match!!!

N.B. Colworth House was the headquarters and Experimental Farm of Lever Bros. the Agricultural Feeding Stuffs Company.

Post War Cricket

April 1945 saw WW11 come to a merciful conclusion and simply everyone breathed a sigh of relief. People began to smile again, with many families being reunited with loved ones, including members of the armed forces being demobbed and evacuees returning home. The pubs were soon beneficiaries of the bon-homie that was generated and a large proportion of the service mens' gratuities disappeared into their tills.

After a couple of weeks celebrating, things gradually returned to normal and those who had been starved of cricket for five years began to look around for a club to join. The grounds at Pertenhall and Kimbolton had not been kept up and would have to wait for another year to be knocked into shape. Lt.Staughton was lucky, in as much as their ground had been kept in order by the RAF, stationed at the local airdrome. The C.O. there was R.E.S.Wyatt, the England captain in the early 1930s and they used the ground for inter-service matches. They were in fact doubly lucky, as the airfield was originally allocated to the USAAF, but it was found that the runways were too short for the B17's and after several near misses, one low flying aircraft knocked the chimney off the local chapel, so it was decided to hand the airdrome over to the RAF, whose Pathfinder Lancaster's could cope with the short runways.

Having relatives in the village gave me sufficient introduction to be included in their team playing in the Bedfordshire league. We probably won a few more matches than we lost but would have been serious contenders in any beer drinking competition.

Watching cricket nowadays, as opposed to playing then, is like comparing chalk with cheese, with such minor inconveniences as bad light and semi-tropical downpours virtually ignored.

Once, when playing at Blunham, a thunderstorm at teatime left the pitch in quite a mess but the game carried on, as we were batting we could not complain. Very soon the creases became churned up and a new batsman, taking guard, let go of the handle and the bat stood upright in the mud!!!

My abiding memory of four happy years with the Club was a Hospital Cup match one evening at North Crawley, which was played in continual drizzle, the home team mustering just 16 runs. We knocked them off in under four overs and were soon in the local to celebrate, with Gordon Robins who had scored most of the runs in fine form. From somewhere he found a doll's pram and to cause a laugh proceeded to wheel it round the bar but he had failed to notice that the biscuit tin balanced on the hood was not part of the structure. On the third circuit the tin fell off and a million buttons cascaded to all points of the compass. The landlord went bananas and there has never been a pub evacuated so swiftly, even during the blitz.

Our bus journey home, interrupted by various breaks, including refuelling, descended into a bout of community singing of old folk songs. This was a popular form of entertainment in those days especially in some of the village pubs. Most of the old songs had an interesting story line woven into them and certainly healthier listening than the doubtful quality of some of the material broadcast today, thinly disguised as entertainment. No wonder the country is going downhill.

Still, nothing stops the same forever and a good thing too, as the combine harvester is certainly a great improvement on the scythe.

No Smoke Without Fire

The recent scandal regarding the horse meat found in products labelled beef does not surprise me in the slightest. Everything in life depends on trust, and with the media able to unearth the truth via mobile phone records or what have you, one wonders if there are any honest people out there. The answer is yes, thank the lord and many of those good souls wonder why the penalties do not fit the crimes.

What Florence Nightingale would have felt about staff at Hospitals where patients were left without food or water cannot be contemplated. The perpetrators should be treated in the same way. When I was a boy, crime was virtually unheard of, with the Magistrates at St Neots Court only having to deal with cyclist riding without lights. The fine would be ten bob, equivalent to one third of a farm worker's weekly wage. Badly behaved children would get a smack from their parents. Now they risk being placed under arrest, from laws made in Brussels that no other country in Europe adheres to.

In the 1950's I played Sunday cricket for St. Neots, who at that time were a good second best to Huntingdon and St. Ives. They had an impressive fixture list including visits to Luton Town, Leicester City Police and the National Westminster Bank up London, secured no doubt because the captain was head of the St. Neots Branch. It was an all day match, travelling up by coach with hot sunny weather helping us along. The result was a high scoring draw. Then down to the important part which was the hospitality, being second to none with free beer afterwards, and we all had far too much, consequently on the way home our bladders came under pressure but the driver took his time before pulling up on Hatfield Market Square. We piled out in complete darkness and finding the Gents proved a bridge too far, so nature took over in what appeared to be a safe rendezvous. Alas PC Plod appeared on the scene and it was a case of the "Devil claiming the hindmost", which was our old Captain who was the slowest runner, and he had his collar felt.

We escaped defeat in the fixture with Leicester City Police by the skin of our teeth mainly because Bill Presland, another Pertenhall stalwart, raked in at the last minute took five wickets and helped to bat out time.

In the canteen afterwards the ante was five bob or 25 new pence with no limit how much anyone ate or drank. Soon after we started home on the coach I began to smell something burning, so the bus was stopped and everyone got out looking for the cause but nothing was found so we set off again, but the smell got worse. Suddenly someone said, "It is you Claude that is on fire!" A spark from my cigarette had fallen down inside my jacket and my tie was smouldering nicely.

No wonder I was the only one to smell it!!!

Two for the Price of One

For a few years after I joined Kimbolton CC in 1953, I began to wonder if I had done the right thing. Having had so much success with our village team at Pertenhall, to be regularly thumped by the opposition at Kym began to wear a bit thin, but when Jeff Hart came from Dean four years later things soon began to improve.

During those early days the conversation centred mainly on the Smith-Barry Cup. This trophy had been donated by the then MP for Huntingdonshire in 1898, and named after him, it is a valuable solid silver rose bowl worth several thousand pounds, to be played for in a knock-out competition by Huntingdonshire teams of amateur players.

Most of the MPs of that era were retired business men who had been successful in trade or commerce and were prepared to give back to the country some of the expertise that had made them wealthy, and for him to donate this wonderful trophy set him on a pedestal. The politicians of today mostly come up through UNI having studied politics and learned not much more than the ability to fill in their expense claim forms. Our present one, apparently a millionaire, claimed £5,000 for security gates, are the vandals any worse at Abbotts Ripton than in other parts of the country? I mistakenly thought those things only happened in Banana Republics.

Anyway, back to the story. Jeff decided we needed to get some good young local players to replace some of the OAP's in the team, and I took on the job of Fall Guy or Recruitment Officer. The first target was Tommy Newman who I tracked down filling his car at Odell's Garage. He did not need much persuading as he was with Huntingdon at the time and they were top dogs then with several playing regularly for the County and Tom was lucky if he got a knock at No.6.

He was working at Thurleigh for the RAE after completing his National Service stationed in Singapore where most of the time was spent playing cricket.

This turned out to be a B.O.G.O.F. deal as not only did we get a top quality all rounder, but his wife Audrey came along to help with the tea rota and is still going strong after 54 years on the treadmill.

Tom's enthusiasm soon saw him elected on to the Committee, at that time fund raising for Pavilion extensions high on the agenda. It was his idea to run a 200 Club and promised to sell 40 tickets. Bill Haley who was doing a grand job running the bar and helping with the ground took 40, so with yours truly chipping in with another 40 the rest of the outfit only had to cope with 80.

At that time it was said the Australian Test team were the first to start sledging (and for those readers not familiar with this terminology,

The "backroom staff" Kimbolton Cricket Club, early 1970's

*Back Row L-R: Michael Bennet, Judy Facer, Bill Haley, Pat Brockman,
Vic Roddis, Bill Presland, Rene Presland, Lionel Sapsed,
Reg (Doc) Facer.*

*Front Row L-R: Gladys Facer, Pat Brown, Barbara Levine, Lil Stringer,
Audrey Newman, Daphne Banks, Betty Lowndes.*

it is what the fielding side is saying to the batsmen to upset their concentration), but Tom must have learned it in the forces because he was able to get up the noses of the opposition to good effect.

In the early days the toilet facilities at the Park were Spartan to say the least with the gents, a V shaped piece of corrugated iron pointing to the SW, the way of the prevailing wind, next to one of the poplar trees round the back. I don't know what some of our town visitors thought of this arrangement because in the cities men often have to travel down into the bowels of the earth before coming up much relieved.

We soon began to find success on the field and everything began to look rosy. The grass was green, the pavilion painted green, the caps were green, but in the early days most things were brown. William was the President, Thomas the Chairman, Ben the Captain and John the fast bowler.

Jeff and Tommy are now looking down on us from their vantage point in the after world, but can rest assured that those of us lucky to be spared another day remember them with affection and appreciation for what they did to help keep the show on the road.

More from K.C.C.

Jeff Hart had played as a guest player several times for Rushden C.C. and had considered joining them, but when he started courting Margaret, one of three Cowlard sisters who lived in the 'Keeper's Cottage', next door to the Park, that probably tipped the balance in favour of Kimbolton. They were soon to marry, following sister Olga to Jim Welton the policeman and Mary to Jeff Hall, son of Les the baker, the latter sister who went on to work for Ron Atzema the Chemist.

One plus sign from his connection with Rushden was that three of their players came to join us at Kimbolton. Bob Marriot an opening bat, Don Freeman a top class wicket keeper and Reg Tobin a good spin bowler. Our cricket at that time was Saturday only playing friendlies, except the Smith Barry Cup where we were usually knocked out in the first round and my debut in the competition resulted in a golden duck LBW Frank Brand at Warboys. So we decided to enter the Bedford Hospital Cup competition, an evening 20 over job and persuaded Jim Gambrel who lived in Bythorn and played for Huntingdon to turn out for us. He was a fearsome bowler and could have walked into Northants County team had his wife been in favour of it.

In 1959 we were lucky with the draw and several early matches were played at home, which helped in putting a decent side together. Eaton Socon were our opponents in the final, one of over a hundred teams who started out, contested in Bedford Park in front of over a thousand spectators. Collections from all games were donated to

Kimbolton 1st X1 Smith Barry Cup Winners, late 1960's

*Back Row L-R: Alan Sivers (Umpire), Evelyn Facer (Scorer),
Tommy Newman, Dai Williams, Malcolm Roddis, Johnnie Walker,
Peter Davison, Ian Burton, Mike Stapleton.*

*Front Row L-R: David Quirke, Bernie Facer, Jeff Hart (Capt),
Robert Davison, Claude Banks, Tony Quirke.*

the Hospital and after the NHS came into being, one year a
television set was bought for the nurses' Common Room.

I was confident enough that we would win to book the
Mandeville Hall for the celebration party and laid on the beer and
refreshments for afterwards and told Dennis Asbury their captain
they all would be welcome whatever the outcome.

As the game unfolded it began to look as if we had twelve players
to their ten as one of their fielders dropped our best opening bat
early on and he went on to get sixty not out. Then when they batted,
the same player ran his captain out in the second over, getting rid of
the one man who might have upset our apple cart.

Recently I came across Eric Oakley their wicket keeper, at
Huntingdon Races and we were able to reminisce on what might
have been.

45

On their way home, one of our Rushden players had a job trying to persuade his car to travel in the direction he was trying to steer it, which resulted in wrapping itself round a keep left sign close to home. Undeterred he walked on and phoned the police the next morning reporting it as stolen.

I hope he did not try that trick too often.

"Getting Caught with Egg on your Face"

A new circle of acquaintances, later on some of them becoming good friends, opened up as I became involved in Hunts County Cricket Club (CCC).

The President Mr Gifford known to everyone as "Uncle George" was a crusty old bachelor farmer from Stukeley and in his heyday played for Huntingdon and Northants CCC as an amateur. His two nephews Macer and Josh were both leading jockeys in the National Hunt world, with Josh stable jockey for Ryan Price the Sussex trainer and between them organised a number of coups in some of the top handicaps.

Macer rode as a freelance jockey and was equally successful and carried on the farm after his uncle retired. Soon after getting married to Sarah, who produced him two daughters who turned out to be pony mad, Macer was struck down with Motor Neurone Disease and to see him wasting away was a sobering experience for us all.

Jeffrey Jones of Ramsey became the Chairman and his deputy Ron Shelley was one of the few that experienced lightening striking in the same place twice. He started farming at Upwood just before the war but lost his land when it was requisitioned for a Pathfinder Air Base. Luckily he was able to rent a farm about the same acreage at Grafham but twenty five years later the Anglia Water Authority decided that would be their site for a new reservoir so Ron had to up sticks again.

The two Brand brothers could not have been more different. Ted was an entrepreneur and started up one of the first vegetable pre-packing plants and became very rich. He always wanted us to join the minor Counties Cricket League and with his new found wealth offered to bankroll our entrance. However our player base was insufficient as the rules stated we had to play a minimum of five two day matches and not one of our players was willing to commit themselves to that extent.

Frank a farmer enjoyed playing cricket and football for his village of Warboys and I remember in a cup semi-final against Kim he was marked by Frank Heading and they spent most of the afternoon kicking lumps out of one another and the referee did not think it worth his while to book either of them.

H.E.P. Grabasky the St Ives dentist was also the Club Treasurer, obviously the idea being that if he could extract teeth, getting donations for the cause would be less painful.

Cyril Asplin our match Secretary, helped run the St Ives market and one Monday morning an OAP who regularly brought in odds and ends came steaming in on his bike with an old hen tucked underneath his arm. Cyril decided to put it in a cage next to a dozen point of lay pullets. Later on when he went round to "lot them up" he noticed one of them had laid an egg, so he took it out and put it in with the old hen, hoping a buyer would bid up and make the old guy an extra bob or two.

Come sale time and as they moved along the line the old hen was next on the list, there she sat in all her glory with a smile on her face and yolk dripping from her beak having just polished off the egg.

Not surprisingly she was knocked down for the maiden bid of half a crown less commission. "Getting caught with egg on your face is better than getting caught with your trousers down"!

How's That?

The bicycle seems to be making a bit of resurgence recently, with several females taking up the challenge. This is good news as not only does it save on petrol it burns up the calories and in time will increase the supply of slim line models and improve the scenery no end. As boys, the bike was our "modus operandi" to school and later on as we grew up, going to dances to meet the girls or as a more earthy terminology "Hunting the crumpet".

The one fact that soon became apparent was the teenage girls often operated in pairs, a pretty girl would have as her companion one quite plain. On a study of human behaviour this made a lot of sense, because the pretty one attracted the boys, which gave her mate a better chance, but not enough to hamper the success rate of the good looking one. Perhaps David Attenborough will do a programme on that subject when he has finished with the animal kingdom.

The sport of cricket has also been renowned for double acts with Hobbs and Sutcliffe, Larwood and Voce, Botham and Willis now Anderson and Broad hitting the headlines.

At KCC early on we had Peter Bance and Dermot Walsh from Sharnbrook to blow away the opposition but later on we had our own home grown pair of wicket takers. Both six feet tall with a high arm action they were a formidable duo. Malcolm Roddis, tall dark and handsome right arm over was a scary sight in the gathering gloom one evening up the park against the Bedford West Indies cricket team in the Hospital Cup. A product of the Pertenhall family, he went to KGS and could have gone to Northants County CC instead he joined the Manchester City Police force then immigrated to Canada where he became successful in the poultry industry.

The other half of the pair, Johnny (Wacker) Walker, no relation to the Whisky distillers, left arm over and deadly accurate. He always bowled with his shirts sleeves buttoned to the wrist but he was told by Jeffrey Jones the Ramsey maestro "Roll your sleeves up Walker and have some snakes tattooed on your arms, then the batsmen will become easy meat".

Johnny worked as a mechanic with Alan Sivers at Phil Parratt's garage; Alan married Brenda Luff whose parents ran the grocery shop in East Street. Her sister Janet married John Williams a farmer from Covington and Tim one of their sons was a useful bowler at KGS. After Uni, he went on to teach at Canterbury from where our

Celebrations at Wornditch Farm, Kimbolton, hosted by Bert and Audrey Bates. Claude has just done "the egg trick!"

go-ahead Headmaster, Mr Belbin started out.

Alan played football and cricket for Kym, a top Club man he was one of the driving forces getting a bar running in the Pavilion and later on becoming a successful umpire, although he tended to side with the batsman over the bowler, to whom he would always explain the reason for "Not Out". "Just missing off" "Pitched outside leg" etc., until one exasperated bowler after having several appeals turned down, pinned the batsman in front with a well directed yorker onto his boot, exclaimed, "I expect that b...r was going underneath".

A Cup of Rosie Lee

Cockney rhyming slang once gave a colourful slant to our language but recently it has virtually died out, although I am a bit of a traditionalist and when the chance arises some gets included in my stories.

One example cropped up during a Committee meeting of the Hunts County Cricket Club for which I was the KCC delegate for over fifty years. About a dozen years into this stint I was elected Chairman, and later on during the treasurer's report we found out the Club was boracic, in other worlds skint after the lint of that name that was used to allay infections in wounds before we started to take pills for everything.

A sub committee was quickly cobbled together to raise funds and for starters we held a 20 mile sponsored walk around Upwood Airfield. This took place on a Sunday morning when it rained most of the time, with all the affiliated Clubs taking part and half the proceeds to the home clubs the rest to the County.

I walked with Jeff and Roger Hart with Jeff the top fundraiser as at that time he drove Fred Mayes the greengrocer's delivery lorry and got all his customers to support the cause. Roger Hart was the Spanish master at KGS and lived in one of the properties in Stonely Hall. This had recently been bought by George Hunt the School Bursar. The previous owners Whitlock-Turner were related to the Welsteads who, with the Duke at one time owned a fair bit of the land and property in this area.

It's a wonder half of us did not go down with the flu after the soaking we got but Roger was so knackered that at night he was unable to climb the stairs and had to sleep under a duvet on the sitting room floor. One saving grace during the walk was the sight of Pat Ruston cruising round in her new blue Mini to help those who had fallen by the wayside. At one time she seemed to have gone AWOL and Roger wondered what was wrong. I suggested she had gone to get filled up with petrol, but Jeff said more likely for a new set of tyres.

A couple of years later we repeated the dose over Wyton Drome and this time the star of the show was Paul Presland. He was a big lad and came home ten minutes before any one else. He was a helicopter pilot in the RAF as well as our best fast bowler and in about 1970 took 4 for 76 playing for the Combined Services against the full West Indies touring team.

Our best effort came next when we joined forces with the Huntingdon Stags Rugby Club and ran a Clay Pigeon shoot on Huntingdon Racecourse. The Stags were mainly farmers' sons and not afraid of a bit of hard graft, so many hands made light work rather than "Too many cooks spoiling the broth", with John Ramply from Southoe and Gweneth Rowlands our new treasurer and Gordon Ashcroft from Yelling, one of the top referees in the Rugby world burning plenty of midnight oil planning the venture.

One big attraction helped as we were able to persuade Gee Armitage the National Hunt champion Lady Jockey to present the prizes. Recently one journalist described a lady tennis player as "Not much of a looker", and found himself submerged in hot water for his trouble. Gee was the opposite and her photo would sit nicely on a box of Cadbury Milk Tray.

Claude with Gee Armitage, Champion Lady Jockey at Clay Pigeon Shoot on Huntingdon Race Course, in aid of Huntingdonshire County Cricket Association Fund Raising

Boiled or Scrambled

Cricket, as most readers by now will have realised, has played a big part of my life, not only as a competitor but later on getting a quiet satisfaction helping to organise.

When the National 50+ Competition was launched in 1984 I managed the Hunts team for the first fourteen years. There was probably more enthusiasm among these players than some of the teenagers in Club cricket, no doubt because it would often be their last "hurrah".

During matches when rain stops play dressing rooms are not usually places of high entertainment but with the old guys getting them to recall amusing incidents that happened in the past would fill several pages, so the following stories are just a sample.

Village cricket where most of us started out was more often than not played in cow pasture fields and Vincent Reed, of Papworth fame, started out as a thirteen year old for Yelling in a match at Little Gransden. The pitch was in a field owned by Dougie Bygraves and the long grass in the outfield had been cut ready to make into hay. Consequently Yelling, who batted first, could not get the ball through to the boundary and were all out for a low score before heading off to the pub for tea. About an hour later they were surprised to find the baler had turned up and cleared the outfield so the home team were able to knock up the runs in record time.

Roy Fage of Sandy told us of the day they turned up to play in a match where a cow had died during the night and lay just where the umpire would stand at square leg. The firm of Beesons at Blunham, whose lorry had broken down, usually collected fallen stock to process in their factory into meat and bone meal to be used as a fertiliser. It was a very hot day and the odour surrounding the unfortunate beast began to get a bit rich so the umpire decided two runs would be awarded to the batting side each time the ball hit the immovable object.

My story of falling in a pond at Thurleigh whilst trying to get under a steepler launched into orbit by one of the Berrill brothers pales into insignificance with one by Dennis Drake the Barnack off spinner. He was one of the few cricketers who took more wickets than he scored runs and during his time in the Army often played in two day inter-service matches. In one of them his side were forced to follow on just before close of play on the first day. Dennis last man in, had failed to trouble the scorers. As they walked off his captain said that with only time for a couple of overs they could go back in and try to do a bit better second time round. But as "Sods Law" would have it, Dennis was castled first ball which gave the sports editor of the local rag a unique head line "Drake gets two ducks".

No Cover Up

Over the years Great Staughton has been fertile ground supplying players for KCC, and soon after Tommy Newman joined I was sent to try to recruit Robert Davison who, with his brother Peter, were playing for St. Neots at the time.

They lived quite near the White Hart in the Highway and one Monday evening saw me knocking on their door. It was answered by his Mother who said he had gone out, but I could come in and have a chat with his father Harry. I was shown into the sitting room where he was reclining on the chaise longue and thinking in that posture he may have been feeling unwell, I apologised for intruding. "Oh no" he said, "I am ok, I am following my grandmother's instructions that Never to stand when you can sit, and never to sit when you can lie".

I have come to see if Robert will come to play for us at Kim I explained. "I wondered when you would turn up and ask" he said "but he won't come unless his brother Peter comes as well." Our captain Jeff Hart said "we had better let him come" although the general opinion at that time was Peter was a spent force having been a fast bowler as a youth and had damaged his back. Now youngsters are only allowed a limited stint which has saved many from these types of injuries.

As it turned out, of the three disciplines in the game, bowling, batting and fielding, Peter joined Robert in opening for the first team and once had a double century stand to win the match. Peter also proved to be a top class close to the wicket catcher especially when Ron Stevenson was bowling his off breaks. He fielded as was known "round the corner" on the leg side, and able to catch with either hand, his arms seemed to stretch like an octopus's tentacles and snaffled up any half chances that were offered.

The brothers were great fun in the dressing room as well as on the field and one day when we were playing Granta our opponents from Cambridge, Bernie Facer was bowling his left arm spinners wide of the off stump with a seven two field. Half way through the over, Jeff, our Captain, said to Peter "go over to the other side" and as he walked across he said, "A couple of you better grease your shoulders and let me come in."

Sadly Robert is no longer with us having joined Jeff, Ron, Tommy, Canon Maurice and all the other players who helped Kimbolton bring home the trophies on so many occasions and, as sure as eggs are eggs, that is a path we will all have to tread at some stage.

My abiding memory of Robert was once when we were playing at Oundle and a violent thunderstorm had flooded the ground at teatime. As we were getting changed, the stumps were marooned on the square and not many go to a cricket match wearing wellingtons. So Robert and yours truly decided to have a race to fetch in one set of stumps each, starkers except holding a towel around our middles. He could run a bit faster than I had bargained for and the only way to get back in front was to let go of my towel. It finished up a dead heat with the first two streakers well and truly out of puff!!.

Kimbolton 2nd X1

Back Row L-R: Dusty Saunders, Paul Carpenter, Michael Bennett, Paul Roddis, Ken Hart, Fred Hart, Frank Squirrel (Umpire).

Front Row: L-R: Maurice Deighton, Keith Diggins, Claude Banks (Capt), Colin Green, Doug Peacock.

The Park

When the next scribe decides to have a go at updating the history of Kimbolton, he or she will first of all have to work out where to start. Will it be the Castle or the range of different building style of various properties on either side of the High Street?

One of the chapters could include the sports area known as "The Park", the home of the cricket and football teams and where it was said that Jack Hobbs the England opening batsman scored his last century.

On another auspicious occasion, soon after the war ended, a cricket match was held to raise money for the "Injured Jockeys

Fund". The Oakley Hunt challenged the National Hunt members who included as well as trainers the top jockeys at the time, David Nicholson and Josh Gifford. A large crowd were spectators and with gifts and raffles a substantial sum was raised for the good cause.

Being a member of an amateur sports team involves more than just turning up to play and for those willing to work together for the cause, helps to build up camaraderie and then success will follow.

Some of my happiest memories are from that tranquil arena away from the hustle and bustle of business life, having become a member of the football club when it was reformed after the war and of the cricket club since 1953. The back drop of the magnificent Wellingtonias give the ground a rather special air and folklore has it that they were planted in 1892 and were the leftovers of the batch that was obtained to plant an avenue from the Portico steps of the Castle to the Bedford Road and beyond into Stonely. The cricket club mindful that they have a life-span, planted in 1976 a dozen or so young trees around them to cater for the enjoyment of future generations.

The cricket club pavilion that nestles so snugly in the corner of the ground also has a great deal of history attached to it. The middle section was once a shepherd's hut, one of several on the estate and Canon Maurice soon after he arrived at Kimbolton, around the turn of the century, persuaded the Duke to have it towed on a wooden sledge by a team of horses and put on a concrete base with a veranda added for good measure.

The 1960's saw the Club forge ahead both on the field and in the committee room with water and electricity being laid on and funds raised to enable a kitchen and toilet to be built on the back and dressing rooms with showers built on either end. With the Cricket World Cup being held in England in 1971 we felt confident enough to challenge the smaller countries who were taking part in a warm-up match before the main event. Papua and New Guinea and Malaysia accepted the invitation and honours ended about even as we lost in the last over to the former and beat Malaysia quite comfortably in the second.

It's not all Club sides that can take on and beat International Teams but to coin a phrase "Those were the days when men were men and women were glad of it".

David One Goliath Nil

It is always nice to receive a surprise invitation, and for me something to do with cricket is a bonus. A couple of summers ago, Thurleigh Cricket Club was holding a celebratory weekend with a couple of matches to mark a milestone in its history.

Having played against them many times, they were always ultra competitive on the field, but later in the pub they were prepared to let their hair down. Since that time they have gone from strength to strength and continue to reach new heights which are bucking the trend where many village clubs have folded and others are struggling.

The trouble maybe lies in the Primary Schools where the enthusiasm to play in team games is not nurtured to the extent of days gone by, with television and mobile phones making couch potatoes out of potential Larwoods and Hobbses.

Half a century ago Thurleigh would have been headline news in the National Press concerning the missing band leader Glen Miller, or as one of the three sites for the new London Airport, but the sports page of the Beds Times would have been following the progress of the village cricket team that carried all before it especially in the Hospital Cup Final of 1958, when they beat Henlow in an amazing game in Bedford Park. Batting second and facing a big total, they lost early wickets before two of the Berrill brothers started to repair the damage, once running two leg byes from a ball that never left the popping crease, before expanding with cover drives that were supposed to be the preserve of Denis Compton.

They played their home matches in a cow pasture field and when Pertenhall were the visitors in about 1950 I was patrolling the long-on boundary when a ball was launched into orbit in my direction. Tall grass and thistles obscured my view as I set off more in hope than expectation and the excuse for failing to take the catch (that I fell in a pond on the way) would get a star rating in "What happened next".

Although names like Asplin and Clayton among others were prominent, the family of Berrill was synonymous with Thurleigh cricket at that time. There were five brothers and if my mind is not playing tricks, Curley, Copper, Bastin, Bomber and Dimmer, were their nicknames.

It was said at the time that Mrs Berrill had the longest clothes line in the country, with so much white cricket gear hanging from it on Mondays it was probably visible from outer space and if the directors of Persil had got to know about it their advertising campaign could have made merry.

Local cricket has always been close to my heart and friendships made along the way have helped to smooth the path ahead.

"Who Dunnit?"

The term "Hat Trick" was supposed to have originated early on when a bowler took a wicket with three consecutive deliveries and was awarded his club cap for the feat. Nowadays when a footballer scores three goals in a match that is also called a "hat trick".

There are plenty of other examples of "Hat Tricks" like when Ian Burton scored a century on three consecutive Sundays up the Park, a feat that I doubt that will ever be repeated. He was the most stylish batsman, without doubt, to play for Kym, his bat was used more as a rapier than a cutlass. Very meticulous in everything he did and as a biology master at KGS he wanted some Brussel sprout stalks for one of his classes to dissect and arranged to be up at the farm at 9am. As a joke I said to him as I opened the door "you are ten seconds late" he replied "It was just nine o'clock when I knocked".

One of the centuries was against Royston when over five hundred runs were scored, another of our team, Mick Taaft and

Nigel Gadsby the opposition captain scored big hundreds as well.

I have also been involved in a hat trick. Like my father and grandfather, head gear has been a must, usually a straw hat in summer and a trilby for winter and outings. Good quality trilbies set you back over fifty quid each and the fact that I have had three pinched, all at cricket events is unusual, expensive and most annoying.

The first was at the Alconbury Hill Hotel owned by Godfrey Horsford and the venue for our County Cricket meetings, a very posh place with a hat stand in the hall where I deposited my trilby and coat, later on to find out that the hat had gone AWOL.

Soon after this happened the hotel was demolished to make way for the upgrading of the A1 into a dual carriage motorway. Godfrey then joined forces with Francis Brand another KGS old boy and started up the very successful enterprise in Huntingdon, Sports and Fashion Store.

The second was at Beadlow Manor Golf Club in Bedfordshire, the occasion a benefit dinner for Alan Lamb, the Northants and England batsman. The cloakroom resembled Fort Knox and should have been safe enough for my new trilby and old mac but alas at the end of the day only the mac remained for me to take home.

The third one to go missing had a touch of Houdini about it as I had migrated to the Alconbury Sports Centre to help with the presentations of the Hunts Cricket Bats Awards evening. Not risking the cloakroom, I placed my hat in splendid isolation on top of the piano where I could keep an eagle eye on it all evening. After leaving the room for a visit to the toilet, when I returned, the hat had gone missing and I thought that one of the lads had hidden it just to wind me up. But no, it had been spirited away.

Whilst I would not want to trouble any one on Crime Watch, Should anyone reading this be able to throw any light on these disappearances it would be most appreciated – all information will be treated confidentially!!!

CHAPTER THREE

Football

Post War Soccer at Kimbolton – Part I

Kimbolton Football Club had no problems restarting after the war as the Royal Army Medical Corps, stationed at the Castle during the War, had used the pitch for inter-service games and had kept it in good order. They also played a couple of matches each season against the local Home Guard, so a nucleus of a team was in place to take over, once hostilities ceased. My best pal at Pertenhall was Ken Gentle. We were both sport mad and 'signed on' for Kimbolton and our names duly went into the hat for the pair of F.A. Cup Final tickets the Club was allocated. As luck would have it, we were the lucky winners, but a relative of the Chairman, who was staying at the Lion Hotel in the village, persuaded us to swap the tickets for a couple of days at his place 'up the smoke' for the VE Celebrations a week or so later.

We had a fabulous time in London, an unforgettable experience that only comes along once in a lifetime. The contrast between dancing the night away in the huge Streatham Locarno, to back on the farm next day, singling out sugar beet, must be somewhere near the opposite ends of any spectrum.

The first match of the football season could not come soon enough, but bone hard ground on a hot day, with strong opposition, showed we were not as fit as we thought we were. Our two-mile home journey, on our bikes, was more like a nightmare than a happy release. Ken was in the worst shape. His boots were not a good fit and bruised his big toes to such an extent, that he lost both nails and had to have a week off work.

We were soon to be strengthened by players returning from the

Services. The first was George Ansell, our Latin master at Kimbolton Grammar School before serving in the Tank Regiment, his nickname at school was 'Killer' and he certainly put opposition to the sword, in one game scoring all the nine goals we won the match by. Les Hewitt a pre-war player, whose ability would have graced a higher stage than the Hunts Junior League, served in the army and played in the away fixture at Somersham where we had to change at the local pub. Les decided to down a double rum before going on to the pitch and since he is now nearly ninety it could not have done him too much harm.

Bob Lilley who had served in the Parachute Regiment returned in time to play in the backlog of fixtures in April 1947, following the extremely bad winter. Coming home on the bus from matches he kept telling us to back 'Airbourn' in the Derby. One evening at the Chequers at Keysoe the bookies runner came in to collect the betting slips, so remembering Bob's advice I had five shillings each way. The horse romped home at 66 to 1 and quite a few recently de-mobbed troops with their gratuities burning a hole in their pockets had lumped it all on the horse and won enough to set them up in house and home. My winnings should have been about £20 plus, about six weeks wages in those days, but the look on the bookies runner's face as he came back into the pub suggested all was not well. He had 'stood the bet' himself thinking the horse could not win and he had not the money to pay up. Negotiations ended with me getting his motorbike instead of money. The bike was a 1926 Model BSA, just my vintage. Everything in the garden was lovely until one night it decided to wrap itself round a telegraph pole and for the few seconds I slithered along the road, I thought we were both going out in the same year, making it a double. Apart from a considerable area of gravel rash and a ruined suit, I escaped with nothing more than dented pride.

Soccer at Kimbolton

Starting off as a small fish in a small pond is the better of the alternatives and beginning with Kimbolton Football Club, a truly amateur club, where all players were expected to be involved in fund raising activities to keep the show on the road, laid the foundations for much enjoyment and satisfaction. Life has shown me that our species is comprised of two distinct categories; those who will do as much as they can and those that will do as little as they need. Fortunately all our team members were of the former category and none more so than Jack Nichols, a farmer from Buckworth who played for Kimbolton at football and cricket. He would look after the young players and sort out any of the opposition bullies who were taking advantage of a lenient referee. He probably weighed less than 10 stone, was made as tough as whitleather and finished each match almost as fresh as he started it. He also bred racehorses and was champion amateur jockey twice in National Hunt Racing, winning both the Cheltenham and Aintree Foxhunter Chases in the same season on 'Lucky Purchase' who was owned by a local grain merchant.

Jim Payne our goalkeeper was probably the shortest player to find himself between the posts but he made up for it in agility and continued to thwart the opposition at crucial times. The name Dicks is synonymous with Kimbolton Football Club and Harry Dicks' goals helped to keep us in many a game when we were struggling. His brother Charlie captained the side with distinction through the 1930's, one of the most successful eras in the Club's history. His wife Barbara has an Aladdin's cave of interesting anecdotes and an hour in her company is more rewarding than several days in the archives of one of the local rags.

Dick Whiteman was *our* captain and although twice our age was very skilful and also knew where to get players when we were short. His family ran the butchers business next door to the Lion Hotel. Dick delivering around the villages in his van while Brother Fred looked after the shop and father, Bill, was the general factotum. Adjoining was another father and son business at the bakery with Les Hall delivering with his horse and cart, although, come the War, he modernised with a motorbike and sidecar. Dick Hall, his father, although well past the first flush of youth arose at 2.30am to prepare and bake the bread.

When France fell in June 1940 several thousand French troops escaped with our boys from Dunkirk together with the young general, Charles De Gaulle, who, at an audience with Mr. Churchill tried to tell him how to run the War. This would have been tantamount to teaching your grandmother how to suck eggs and Winston told him to 'something off' sooner rather than later. He took the hint and cleared off to Senegal the French protectorate in West Africa. Dick, reading the newspaper headlines to Bill at breakfast the next morning remarked that De Gaulle had gone to Dakar. Bill replied, "Did Les take him in his sidecar"?

Old jokes, unlike good wine, do not improve with keeping but in those desperate days, when good news was hard to come by, that one echoed round the area and helped lift morale almost as much as some of Mr. Churchill's speeches.

Summing up, playing sport is a good opportunity for youngsters to mix with like minded characters and creates a medium for exercising the body and building friendships that stand the test of time.

More from Kimbolton Football Club
1951 – 52

After several years in the Hunts League it was decided to enter the Rushden and District competition. Why, I am not sure, as it involved travelling to Grendon and Wellingborough which seemed as far as Yaxley and Ramsey previously. However, a change of scenery added extra to the memory bank and our fist visit to Rushden was quite amusing. We were due to change at "The Adult School" but after riding around in circles for some time the coach driver decided to pull in and ask one of the locals, who pointed to a sign on the building just above our heads in two foot high lettering "Rushden Adult School". Yes, the country bumpkins had arrived in town.

We had to start off in the second division which was far below

Hunts League standards and finished up runners-up in the first season and winners the next season, so on most Saturday evenings we were drinking "winning" beer. At about that time the social scene in Kimbolton was also going through a change with a new landlord at the Lion turning out to be a damp squib and with Roger and Eileen Dunkley installed at The George they became the beneficiaries of most of the trade, including the cricket and football crowd. Ex RAF, Philip Parratt was one of the last to be demobbed and known as P.Y.P., a larger than life character who could see the funny side of any situation and fitted into both the cricket and football teams. Living close to the George, he was soon challenging for the title of court jester especially on Saturday evening celebrations. One or two of the old customers did not take kindly to their sedate games of dominoes being interrupted and loudly proclaimed that they were sick and tired of hearing about us winning. As quick as a flash P.Y.P. said that we were the ones who were "sick and tired of winning" and a new catch phrase was born that lasted for close on twenty years.

Reg Facer was our linesman and known as "Doc" because he also carried the magic sponge, the "cure all" for cuts and bruises. He was a handy chap to have around especially on the occasions the driver had time for us to grab a meal at a café on the way home. Reg's appetite was legendary and cleared up any chips or peas or whatever else was left over. Reg was also a keen fisherman and on Sunday mornings often took his young son, Bernie, with him to the deep pools along the River Kym, which held stocks of large pike. On one occasion, he had taken a good old lump of dough as bait, being easier to prepare than digging for worms, but as everyone knows fishing is not an exact science and what works one day is unlikely to the next and so it proved. With the prospect of the morning spent without so much as a bite, Reg asked for some more bait. "There is none left Dad". "Well where has it gone"? "I have eaten it", admitted Bernie which shows there is still some mileage left in the old saying "like father, like son".

Kimbolton Football X1 around 1950

Back Row L-R: Philip Parratt, Bob Lilley, Dick Hawkins, Alan Sivers, Snowy Gentle, Roy Bruce John Mayes, Doc Facer.

Front Row L-R: Philip Hart, Pat O'Callahan, Brian Whitlock, Jeff Hart, Claude Banks.

Mud, Mud Glorious Mud

For somewhere that is at least six miles as the crow flies from Pertenhall it seems strange that the village of Souldrop has appeared so frequently on my radar. The first time, in 1930, as a small boy living with my grandparents at Manor Farm I spent many hours with the men tending the livestock, and one day the old shepherd said "listen boy, you can hear the trains at Souldrop, so it will rain tomorrow". In those days most country people were well clued up as to what the weather might do and a gentle breeze from the South West meant rain was on the way and to hear the trains at Kimbolton Station to the North was a sign of a spell of fine weather to come.

At that time steam was still the motivational force and the noise heard from the stations would be the trains shunting the goods wagons in and out of the sidings, with mainly coal coming in, and local produce loaded for distribution. The only competition to the noise level would have been from animals and birds as aircraft and road traffic had yet to make a significant appearance.

During the period just before and after D. Day we took our turn in the Home Guard, doing night duty, protecting the LMS railway tunnel against possible sabotage. A few years later, as one of a team of guns invited to Souldrop, to a shoot on a brilliant day, weather wise, with new territory to explore and good company, it was just a shame the birds were conspicuous by their absence and the only bonus, is still being around to tell the tale.

Heavy overnight rain had left the pitch in a sorry state for our visit to Souldrop in the Rushden Football League in the early 1950's and our defence was well master of their lightweight attack, especially the young centre forward who took plenty of stick and by the end of the match the only part of him not covered in mud was the whites of his eyes. Twenty years later at the farm one morning a rep from the local grain merchant arrived looking for business. Over a cup of tea we were soon talking sporting memories and as he came from Souldrop that match was given an airing, and by now you will have guessed correctly, he was the young centre forward.

Those who have taken part in team sports usually find it easy to make friends, which is hard luck on inner city children whose playing fields were sold off for development, and with the chance of employment when they leave school receding, the old saying, "The devil makes work for idle hands," rings only too true.

CHAPTER FOUR

School Days

Spare the Rod

Dinners were not available at Pertenhall C of E School when I started in January 1930 so I used to run the three quarters of a mile to Manor Farm for lunch and was accompanied by another farmer's son who lived close by. Grandmother always had my meal ready and I was back at my friend's house well before they had finished which gave me time to study the surroundings. The kitchen was typical of most in those days and doubled up as the living room, with a cast iron coal fired cooking range providing plenty of heat, above it at ceiling height a cross beam hanging from which were half a dozen or so hams and sides of bacon enclosed in white pillow cases labelled with dates of origin so they could be used in the correct order.

The dining table was directly below a hefty central beam that presumably kept the bedroom above from responding to the force of gravity and a series of nails along either side held a number a number of essential items for the day to day running of the household, the most important a paraffin lamp, electricity not arriving until 1945. On one side a twelve bore hammer type shotgun was at the ready in case a prospective meal presented itself in the orchard and on the other side a horse whip just above the farmer's chair.

Running a business is about selling your product at (hopefully) a percentage more than the cost of the input and in the 1930's St. Neots market on a Thursday was the place for the farming community to go come Hell or High water. Shaw's sale rooms coped with plants and vegetables, butter and eggs, poultry, game and much more. Ekins auction dealt with all livestock, fat and store, through

Pertenhall Infant School 1930

Back row L-R: Jim Clark, Maureen Clarke, Sidney Shelton, Raymond Clarke, Gladys Reynolds, Fred Braybrook.

Front Row L-R: Edna Nicholson, Bob Roddis, John Shelton, Claude Banks

the sale ring and in the Corn Exchange merchants were at their desks to price up samples of grain and oil seeds as well as offering artificial fertilizer and imported livestock feed for forward delivery.

Wives often went along to the shops and took advantage of any bargains to be had at stalls on the market square.

So the scene was set, Thursday lunch time and I was back at my friend's house but tension filled the air, the boy wanted to go to market with mum and dad but they were adamant that he went back to school. We have all seen children trying it on but this one went too far when he lay on his back kicking his legs in the air and screaming at the top of his voice. Father calmly got up and reached for the horsewhip whereupon Sonny Boy stopped crying and shot out of the door at the speed of a Flying Bomb leaving its launching ramp, down the lane they went at a rate of knots with me following on at a safe distance.

I don't think he ever intended hitting the boy and the operation has reminded me of countries that test fire missiles to let their neighbours know they could mean business.

From the cradle to the grave, life is one long learning curve, no one can always be right and a deterrent must be in place for orderly situations to prevail and loving parents and guardians should know best when a persuader is necessary.

Smacks on my backside hurt the pride more than the flesh.

At Pertenhall School

One Saturday morning, in the Easter holidays of 1936, three Pertenhall boys set off to sit the entrance examination for Kimbolton Grammar School. Our journey was interrupted by the Kimbolton post lady, who considered it her duty to jay walk across the road and all traffic was expected to give her the right of way. One of our mates was on his mother's bike which was far too big for him. This was the irresistible force that hit the immovable object, the post lady, amidships, outside the Mandeville Hall and they both ended up beneath the bike.

We had been well prepared by our school-mistress Mary Mason, a farmer's daughter from High Park Farm situated midway between Stonely and Easton, up a long muddy track which was considered locally to have been one mile from nowhere. Miss Mason was quite tall and thin, with her hair scraped into a bun on the back of her head and her sole aim in life seemed to be, that her charges would learn what she taught come hell or high water. To emphasise a point she would raise her voice until she frothed at the mouth and if this did not work she would stamp her foot so hard that one day it went clean through the floor boards. Not satisfied with just learning the three R's, the boys had to do raffia work and basket weaving and the girls, knitting and sewing.

Nature study was a must, the contents of jam jars on the window sills kept pace with the seasons and frog spawn, hairy caterpillars and a multitude of insects did their stuff under close supervision and seeds germinating in trays, with mustard and cress on blotting paper, I suspect added flavour to Miss Mason's lunch time sandwiches.

During those winter's heavy snowfalls were quite common and one morning we awoke to six inches of the white stuff, which, we thought, would put paid to Miss Mason's bicycle journey and we were looking forward to the infant's teacher being in charge, so that when the cat was away, the mice could play. However, Miss was no shrinking violet and turned up as usual, but on her father's hunter – when the going gets tough, the tough get going.

The Exam lasted about a couple of hours, with a short break half way through. It was mainly maths in the first part and general knowledge and current affairs after the break, during which the master in charge called each boy up to read a short passage from a novel, followed by the question, "Why do you want to come to Kimbolton School?" This was not part of the script and my answer, "Because you have some nice cricket pitches to play on", was the first thing that came to mind.

Twenty boys were successful and started at the school at the beginning of the autumn term. Our classroom was in the old chemistry lab, complete with Bunsen Burners still connected to the supply from the gas works down 'The Carnaby'. Mission was accomplished when selected to play for the Under 13's the following summer versus Bedford Modern School and our captain was Frank Chamberlain a family member of the Rushden leather manufacturers. Later in life he was elected Chairman of the Test and County Cricket Board at Lords and this, at the time, gave him top spot for local sporting achievements. Frank retired to live in Swineshead and I was able to visit him in hospital whilst he recovered from a hip replacement operation, which provided us both with an opportunity to swap experiences. Frank spent some time at Uppingham School, after Kimbolton and then went straight into the Fleet Air Arm and then saw active wartime service, flying fighter planes off aircraft carriers, escorting three Arctic convoys to Russia. That must rank alongside the most hair-raising experiences ever. The odds on returning from one of those sorties were only 50-50, but to come back intact from three missions was on par with winning the lottery.

Frank Chamberlain and Mary Mason both came from completely opposite environments and had very different lifestyles, but one of the things they had in common was the ability to influence those around them to go on to better things.

Great Staughton School around 1930 in playground at the back of the old school

Back row left to right – Mary Mason (teacher), Stan Bailey, George Boston. Jack Matthews. Arthur Jakins, Percy Moyser (policeman's son), Jim Dawkes, John Hawkins.

Middle row – Eileen Standen, Joan Nagle, Enid Boston, Millie Button, Jean Hackett, Marjorie Peacock, Violet Besworth.

Front Row- Kathleen Caley, Susan Hackett, Dennis Day, Tony Lovitt, Mary Davison, Blanche Mansfield, Arthur Pickering, John Willmer.

Happy Days

The boys cycling down the B660 to Kimbolton Grammar School in the 1930's were among the few who did not dislike Monday mornings, as this was the era when the motor car was taking over from the horse and weekends were the time to enjoy this new mode of transport. Those motorists heading east, after negotiating the four right-angled bends in Kimbolton saw the straight road along the causeway as an opportunity to make up for lost time. However, the hump-backed bridge, over the River Kym at Stonely, was a problem, made worse by the road veering sharply to the right immediately after it and vehicles hitting the bridge travelling at 40 mph or more became airborne and when they returned to earth landed on top of the hedge or nose first in a deep ditch. Not many Mondays went by when the boys did not find a car in this predicament and were highly amused; especially the boy whose daily round trip from Odell was a cool 27 miles.

As the War got underway, petrol rationing meant that one thing that made school life bearable, the inter-school sporting fixtures were now being cancelled and a period of boredom set in. Making mischief to relieve boredom was not a good option as minor infringements of the rules resulted in having to write out hundreds of lines, which was time consuming and any worse misdemeanour like getting caught smoking behind the bike sheds triggered an invitation to visit the headmaster's study. Mr. Ingram was a foreboding character and not a person to 'get on the wrong side of' and those that did were reckoned to have suffered a fate worse than death.

Light relief came when a family, which had escaped from France, had their son accepted at the school and the boy travelled to and fro with the gang. The big moment came when we were coming home one afternoon and half way down Chapel Hill the local farmer decided it was time to take his cows across the road for milking. The regular boys had coped with this many times before but Raymond

Straal found out, too late, that his brakes were not up to scratch. After hitting one cow broadside on, cleared the rest of the herd and when the force of gravity finally came into play his contact with the road resulted in several days on the sidelines recovering from gravel rash, whilst his bike was being reassembled.

The summer we were due to sit our School Certificate Examination coincided with the army taking over the Castle, and one enterprising squaddie, examining the contents of the library, came across a lengthy poem that colourfully described the progress of a troupe of 40 can-can girls touring the Wild West and their encounter with a couple of gun-touting out-laws. Someone with access to a typewriter did a goodly trade at 6d per copy and I expected, at any time, to find out that they were to be confiscated. One of the books in our English Literature Syllabus was "Macbeth". The only thing of note I can remember of it was that three of the characters took great delight in arranging their rendezvous to coincide with adverse weather conditions. Not surprisingly, of "Eskimo Nell", I can remember quite a bit more and had that been in the syllabus the pass rate would probably have been much higher.

The 1935 Buildings Kimbolton School

Kimbolton Grammar School 1936 – 41

There was no set of rules and regulations for us to follow, as we parked our bikes and proceeded to the Old Lab. If we were expecting a stroll in the park, as opposed to Miss Mason's no thrills approach, we were soon to realise that we had jumped out of the frying pan into the fire. The form room was just off the main corridor, half way between the head master's study and his residence, the Bungalow, so every day he passed by at least half a dozen times and would often look through the window over the door to see if we had our noses to the grindstone. He was an imposing figure with heavy features and large horn-rimmed spectacles and the sight of him peering at us was very much like being watched by a large bird of prey.

To say that he ruled with a rod of iron would be putting it mildly and everyone was in awe of his presence. The punishment of being sent to his study was considered to have been a fate worse than death, although he never needed to resort to the use of the cane. The verbal roasting was such that not many trod that path a second time. The day boys had nick named him 'the old man' and the boarders, 'King' and looking back over the years and reading his book a couple of times, the second description was nearer the mark. He was 25 years old when he was accepted as junior master in 1912 and quickly realised that there were serious problems regarding the school's viability, with less than thirty pupils and a Head Master, whose health was in serious decline, so much so, that Inspectors were soon on the scene and decided that the Head should tender his resignation.

Mr. William Ingram was the governors' choice of over 100 applicants and must have shown the potential needed to rescue a school that had been going for over three hundred years. The school first started in a building on the west side of the church yard before moving to where the Prep School is now. At that time everything had to be squeezed into not much more than one acre of space, with football and cricket matches played on the town ground in The Park. The prospect of being able to attract more pupils, under these

74

Kimbolton School Sports Day 1937
– Claude centre stage with hands in pockets.

circumstances, looked bleak. Succeed he did and almost without exception, the many thousand of boys who benefited from being educated under his regime would agree that strong discipline in the formative years gives a sound foundation for successful careers.

When we started in 1936 the numbers had risen to 250, with playing fields on both sides and the potential for successive headmasters to exploit, so that now, Kimbolton School is one of the leading Public Schools in the country. In his younger days William Ingram played cricket and football for the Town whenever he could spare the time away from school, which underlines the old saying 'all work and no play, makes Jack a dull boy'!!

Life was certainly never dull when William Ingram was around.

Walking the Walk at Kimbolton Grammer School

Our intake of twenty scholarship day boys in September 1936 was made up of half coming in on the Raunds and Thrapston buses and the rest on bicycles, Robert Hellet, Sid Staff and Bob Kitely from Kimbolton, John Shelton and yours truly from Pertenhall, Brian Baker, Perry and Dick Hawkins from Great Staughton, John Hartop from Keysoe and Dick Lack Colesden and Roly Nickleson from Melchbourne.

At the end of each term we were given an envelope to take home. The contents were résumé of our term's work plus a bill. Mine was 7/6d or 37½ new pence. The breakdown, 5/- for books, 2/6 for sport, which took a bit of working out as each week we had only two periods of sport, two of P.E. and thirty one of lessons. I still have my school blazer made at Carnaby House by Mr. Foskitt and son Jamie wore it during his time at KGS in the early 70's.

One of the first hiccups came on the evening of November 5th when the boarders were returning to their dormitories in the town and were ambushed at the bottom of Pound Lane by a gang of local boys with several salvos of fireworks. According to reports all hell was let loose for a while with the police also involved. The next morning we were just taking our first lesson when "you know who" walked in and one of the three Kimbolton boys was taken out of class. Apparently he had been one of the culprits but was allowed back after a couple of days "cooling off".

The amazing thing about Ingram was his ability to detect events almost as soon as they happened, as though there were a series of hidden surveillance cameras beaming pictures onto a screen in his study. One lunch time Ken Hudson from Stanwick climbed up to the swallow nests in the boys toilet block, using the water cistern to haul himself up, which came away and smashed to smithereens on the concrete floor. By the next morning he was on the carpet and faced expulsion unless his father paid for the damage.

Without any shadow of doubt the most hated event was "The Walk" which took place on Wednesday afternoons when the playing fields were water logged. The whole school took part and the route always the same, right out of the gate, left up the Thrapston road to the top of Bustard Hill and back through Tilbrook, a distance of over 3½ miles.

The rules were; only two abreast, no running and starting times staggered to avoid congestion. Several prefects were expected to keep an eye open for trouble makers and 'W.I' would cruise stealthily round in his car. The traffic level in those days was minimal and we would have been nearly the last to take part in this seemingly sadistic keep fit charade, as the weather was always vile with an east wind and drizzle that permeated both body and soul.

One little gang thought it would be clever and slipped through the fields from the bottom of the hill into Tilbrook cutting off the worst part, but after one successful outing the next time "The Old Man" was waiting for them as they crept through the hedge. I am not sure what he said to them but should there be any left to tell the tale, I am sure it would be most interesting.

More from Kimbolton Grammar School

There is no doubt that our country is in a good old mess at the moment, with the tax payer having to come to the rescue of the Banks and it is not only the financial crisis that is the problem. Many parents whose children are at inner-city comprehensives are concerned that they will leave school with inadequate qualifications to cope with the next stage in life. One of the obvious reasons for this must be that the number of hours spent in class is far less than in our era but I am sure neither the pupils nor the teachers complain about the week long half terms as well as three or four weeks at Christmas and Easter with a couple of months in the summer for good measure.

During our time at KGS, only those pupils who were up to scratch with their work were allowed a half day off mid-term and in June 1938, Mr. Ingram came into our form room just before lunch time and spoke to the master and yours truly was one of the lucky ones. "Banks, is your father hay-timing?" "Yes Sir". "Then you can go and help him this afternoon." Pick-up balers had not been invented at that time and my job was to drive the tractor straddling the swaths, towing a wagon behind which was hitched to the hay loader, an ingenious machine that scraped up the crop with a series of rakes and tines and pushed it up a sloping floor dumping it on the wagon. Extension sides had been added to them to increase capacity and make it easy for the loaders as with a thick crop or the driver going too fast the nickname 'man killer' given to the hay loader became obvious. It was a stinking hot day and every time a fork full was pushed to the front of the wagon a shower of dust and hay seeds came down my neck and with every fly in the North Bedfordshire intent on landing on any patch of bare skin, I remember thinking how much better life would be, back in the class room.

Rabbits were a problem on the school playing fields at that time and although wire netting round by the woods helped, some still found their way in and three boarders were upgraded to warreners and set traps and snares to keep them in check, which during the wartime produced welcome additions to the food supply.

One lunch time two of us day boys were caught fooling around in the classroom by Mr. Gibbard, who was on duty that day. He was the second master, having already been at Kim a year when Mr. Ingram turned up in 1912. We were given the punishment of having to learn the 113 psalm and report to him in a week's time. The irony was, having learnt it off pat and reporting to him, as requested, he said he did not want to hear it. He certainly knew how to turn the screw and one of his favourite sayings was "you can't do maths, neither could your father or your grandfather". Not many masters stay long enough to teach two generations let alone three.

I usually had lunch with my Aunt who lived opposite the bakery and after a couple of years she asked me if there was anything I particularly liked as she was having a problem with the menu. Wartime rationing let me off the hook because I said pork chops were quite nice and for the next year or so we had them nearly every day and now I would much rather have a cheese and pickle sandwich.

Spilling the Beans

We, as dayboys were probably the lucky ones of all the pupils at KGS during William Ingram's reign because at least we could live a more normal life when we arrived home. He was virtually a dictator and had total control over all and sundry with masters forbidden to use the local pubs. The only exception was Mr. Gibbard or "Bant" as he was known to all the boys. Mr. Gibbard was house master to the boarders in "Kimbolton House". After they were safely bedded down he slipped across to "The George Hotel" and regularly had a couple of pink gins, but not in the bar or lounge. There was a small hatch in the passageway that opened behind the bar and he spent just a short time there enjoying his tipple.

Most people before the war travelled by bicycle, and those masters that felt in need of extra company and the light relief that alcoholic stimulus can provide, migrated to the "White Horse" at Tilbrook or "The Crown" at Little Staughton. Whereas the Northampton Brewery beer at Tilbrook was well in advance of the Charles Wells at The Crown and much nearer. The one at Little Staughton became the favourite mainly due to the landlord, Billy Lumbers being the ideal "Mine Host".

Quite a number of boys did not take too well to the stringent regime and recently several O.K.'s★ have expressed their dissatisfaction, but as far as I was concerned those that kept their heads down and got on with their work were not inconvenienced. In any case when we are young, that is the time to be under strong discipline, then it stays with you for ever and you are more likely to keep to the straight and narrow path.

One of W.I's saving graces was his love of sport, which was compulsory at the school and any ne're-do-well needed permission from Matron to miss games, however foul the weather. Several masters regularly played for the Town at cricket and a photo of the successful Kimbolton side, captained by Canon Maurice in 1936 with The Smith Barry Cup in front of them included both Kyffin Owen and Willie Watson the Geography master.

Parents who had horses in training soon became friendly with W.I. and when one was favourably handicapped and likely to do the business he got to know and placed a bet accordingly. Whether he passed the message on to the other masters is doubtful but some of them were interested enough in the "Sport of Kings" to bicycle to Saturday meetings at Newmarket, as in those days the School operated a five day week.

Later on three of us lads also took up the challenge, but once only, no problem on the way there with a tail wind to help, but the journey back, although considerably lighter in the pocket was a reminder that at times "Discretion is the better part of valour".

★*O.K's – Old Kimboltonians*

Why is the Sky Blue?

When we were children we were constantly being reminded that our school days would be our best days but that took a bit of believing as in the winter bedtime was at seven o'clock. In the summer we were allowed to stay up later, the reason no doubt because we had to shut the hens up and they never went to roost until it got dark.

Nothing much changed when we started at Kimbolton Grammer School, with the dreaded prep (homework) that hung like the Sword of Damocles over those who failed to keep up to scratch. But before long instead of sweating blood at home we set off half an hour earlier in the mornings and did it in the form room before going in to assembly.

The two periods of sport per week to a non academic outdoor type, was like a shot in the arm to a junky awaiting his next fix and the lure of a whole afternoon off lessons by getting selected to play for one of the school teams the ultimate goal.

I was lucky in as much as my favourite subject was geography, Mr. Watson the master was also the one in charge of the under 13's and 14's cricket XI's, so I naturally tried to keep on the right side of him. He was no doubt aware of this and made sure I kept awake during his lessons because one day when climate was the subject under discussion and the way it affected food production, he went on to say "Weather forecasting is beneficial to fishermen and farmers, isn't it Banks!" I replied, "It probably was more useful to fishermen than farmers". "Can you explain why?" was his retort. "Well sir, for fishermen to go on a long trip if gales were forecast would not be a wise thing to do, but for farmers they cannot do their work until the time comes and then the weather is there." One up to me, but he was not long in squaring the circle.

Sometime later in another geography period he said, just before the bell, that we were all well up with our work and had anyone a question they would like to ask. Of course we all sat there like stuffed dummies and he said "come along surely someone can think of a problem that needs solving", upon which one boy put his hand up and said "Please sir, why is the sky blue", and I burst out laughing. I was immediately brought down to earth when Mr. Watson said "that is typical of you Banks to laugh at something very significant, because there is a reason for everything and the reason why the sky is blue is…", but by this time my mind was in turmoil having been slapped down in front of my mates that my brain stopped working for a while and I cannot remember the answer. If anyone does know 'why the sky is blue' – please stop me and tell me, because it has been bugging me for over 75 years!

A Worthy Role Model

Talking to others of our age group, we have more trouble remembering what we did yesterday than when we were children, as though we are looking through the wrong end of a telescope.

There is also less respect nowadays with politicians fiddling the till with their expense claims and the police with their deceitful reporting of the Hillsborough football disaster.

All children, when we were young, went to Church or Chapel every Sunday morning and Sunday School in the afternoon and were taught the faith that there is a spiritual life after death and the Holy Trinity are the umbrella Christians shelter under, especially when things start to go wrong.

There have been other Trinities or threesomes in the past, with Churchill, Roosevelt and Stalin during the war plotting the downfall of the Axis Powers. More locally, we had our own big three, and for close to half a century William Ingram, Canon Maurice and Alderman William Brown of Covington provided the stability that is lacking in the country if listening to the BBC News is anything to go by.

Whereas Ingram was content to make sure his charges were provided with an education sufficient to cope with the trials and tribulations of the years ahead, Canon Maurice took it upon himself to care for his flock with more than just their spiritual needs. He also captained the cricket team and ran the gas works as well as chief of the Fire Service and his idea that a committee should consist of three members, two of which took turns in not turning up came second in originality only to the invention of the wheel.

William Brown was one of the very few to have the uncanny knack of running a farming business successfully, even when times were bad. He was aware that the three certain ways of losing money are slow horses, fast women and trying to fatten cattle in straw yards during the winter.

His policy of using a contractor with steam engines to pull up his land as soon as the crop had been harvested enabled him to keep ahead of the ball game. By the time he was thirty he was farming fifteen hundred acres as well as running a butchers' business, but found time to become a Local Councillor and was made Chairman of the Thrapston Branch. A few years later, he was elected on to the Hunts County Council and became head of the Road Improvement Committee. These somewhat onerous tasks soon appeared child's play as to what followed when WWII broke out.

He was a member of the War Ag. under Sir Richard Proby which was responsible for bringing back into production thousands of acres that had become derelict. He was then head of the Tribunal that adjudged the amount of manpower each farm should be allowed. This task was made slightly easier as of his four sons, Thomas, the eldest, was now running the farm and the other three had volunteered for the armed forces, although John was refused on the grounds that food production was paramount. Ben went into the Air Force and was badly wounded when his plane was shot down in North Africa, just after Alamein. Jim, the second youngest, whose athletic ability saw him win the mile race twice on KGS Sports days, sadly lost his life in the Burma campaign.

William had a close affinity with KGS starting in 1896 as one of only 28 pupils, leading on to become Chairman of the Governors from 1956/66 as the school went from strength to strength like a Phoenix emerging from the ashes of almost certain closure, owing to lack of numbers, to one of the most sought after co-educational centres outside Oxbridge.

There have possibly been, in the past, those with a similar amount of drive and ability, but not many who have channelled so much of it for the benefit of their fellow men.

A Fortunate Breakdown

I was one of twenty Scholarship day boys that started at Kimbolton Grammar School in September 1936. The Old Lab was our form room and during my five years there, three of them were spent in the 1927 building which was used for our entrance exam and also for our Cambridge School Certificate.

Now retired I live about thirty yards from Ashfield House which was Mr. Ingram's retirement home and where he wrote his book "The Power in a School". In it he describes the fight he had to keep the school going and finally set in motion the foundation for much that has happened since.

The Old Laboratory classroom

One amusing passage involved the purchase of an "Adams" car which had a chain drive that occasionally came apart and was left lying snake like on the road. What he did not mention was that it happened in Great Staughton on a day when he was going to catch the train at St. Neots for an important meeting up in London. Luck was on his side for once because it was right outside George Matthews' blacksmiths shop. He took Mr. Ingram to the Station on his motorbike and sidecar, mended the chain and fetched him back from the Station later on.

George Matthews son Jack★, about four years older than me, also went to KGS and Mr. Ingram secured him a four year apprenticeship at Allens Engineering Works in Bedford.

However two years in, the war had broken out and Jack was enlisted into the Army.

After demob he finished his apprenticeship and rose through the ranks to be Head of Quality Control. He belonged to the Bedford Lodge of Free Masons and visited the branch at Kimbolton from time to time; he left a lasting impression on those who were privileged to have known him.

Sadly Jack is no longer with us but the large number of old boys and ex masters at his funeral service were able to pay their tribute to an extra ordinary person who always put others first.

The tranquil atmosphere in the Ashfield area has given me the incentive to pen some of my memoirs.

Let's keep our fingers crossed for a following wind.

See Jack Matthews in the photograph of Great Staughton Primary School, together with the teacher, Mary Mason, who became Claude's much loved teacher at Pertenhall Primary School a couple of years later.

CHAPTER FIVE

Second World War

Growing up During the War

The period of complacency that had set in from September 1939 to the spring of 1940 was rudely awakened by the Blitzkrieg that had conquered most of Europe by the end of June and left us alone against the might of Germany and Italy. Our Prime Minister, Mr. Churchill, had several times contacted Mr. Roosevelt, The American President, to come in on our side. "I would love to Winston", he said, "but the Senate won't let me". The simple truth was that they did not want to back a loser, which to all intents and purposes we were. But what they had not taken into account was:-

The English Channel.

The wise decision of our Air Force Command that had kept back a few hundred fighter planes and pilots, which would certainly have been lost had they been committed to the futile attempt to save the fall of France.

Mr. Churchill's 'never say die' spirit that refused to surrender and sue for peace with Rudolph Hess, the envoy that Hitler had parachuted into Scotland, which most of the British Cabinet wanted him to do.

A civilian force was gathered together in a matter of days to help combat the threat of invasion. This was soon to be known as the Home Guard and as no rifles were available, twelve bore sporting shotguns were provided with ammunition whose projectile was one ball bearing which if fired would probably have split the barrel of the gun and since the range of that type of gun is not much more than 60 yards the omens were not looking good. I was not old enough to join but managed to take my father's place on the Fire Watching rota that came round about once every couple of weeks. There were three members each night and I found it extremely boring as nothing ever seemed to happen.

My life had been mapped out for me as soon as I started at Kimbolton Grammar School in 1936. I was to be trained in auctioneering because the outlook for farming at that time was a life of hard work, followed by almost certain bankruptcy. I started at Thrapston at the end of 1941 and if I thought fire watching was boring, that had nothing on sitting in an office from 9am to 5pm. The only respite was Tuesday market day, the odd farm sale and the three day sale of the contents of Lilford Hall which had been commandeered for the war effort. The experience however, served me well, in that looking back it taught me not to expect jam on everything and many times I offered up a silent prayer that Dad could see that I was not happy and after a year he brought me back on the farm.

As soon as I reached 17 most of my school mates were in the armed forces and I decided to go and volunteer. Giving my name and address to the Enlisting Officer he asked what work I was doing. "Driving a tractor on my father's farm", was my answer. He looked up and said, "My boy, this country has only six weeks food supply left, the U-boats are sinking our ships faster than they can be made and we are more likely to lose the war from starvation than in any battle. You will serve your Country better on your tractor than by driving a tank". I must say I was a bit relieved, as telling Dad I had joined up would have released a torrent of invective that he specialised in when put out, that included a combination of all known swear words and some new ones he seemed capable of inventing on the spur of the moment. So it was farm work plus the Home Guard to occupy myself and it was no use thinking about girls because the Yanks had the supply well catered for. There was no sport either and life in a monastery might for some have had its attractions.

Our Home Guard chief was a retired Army Officer, almost a

carbon copy of Captain Mainwaring of Dad's Army. He had served in India and retired as Major General but when reaching the age of 70 no one could hold rank and he then became Private Major General Lock. He took us out one night on exercise up the fields and everyone got completely lost as with cloud cover and the black-out, darkness was complete. When the Italian prisoner killed his guard and escaped into the woods, we had to spend the night in the open and in the period before and after D Day, we had to take turns in guarding the main LMS railway tunnel at Souldrop, in case it was sabotaged, which would have severely hampered invasion plans. One Sunday in May 1944 a big exercise was held nationwide by the Home Guard and we had to report to Pertenhall School at 5am. Some of us were sent on our bicycles to help the Kimbolton Home Guard mount a mock attack on the Castle. Our platoon was to advance from the direction of the 'Owen Cricket Pavilion'. Crawling along on our bellies, through the long grass and about half way there an umpire stepped out of the bushes and said "you five have been shot". We said thank you very much, got on our bikes and went home for breakfast. To be umpired out at cricket is the worst possible scenario but in battle, certainly the best!

More from the War

The early weeks of WW11 did not create the excitement a thirteen year old boy expected and the initial buzz, created by the arrival of the London evacuees, soon waned. As if to oblige and liven things up, the first bombs to drop in Bedfordshire fell at Pertenhall in October '39, but thankfully, no damage was done.

1940 saw most of Europe overrun and with the U-boats knocking on our door, the food rationing added impetus to the slogan "Dig for Victory" and lawns and flowerbeds made way for growing vegetables. Derelict farmland was brought back into production and game shooting was virtually discontinued. The humble rabbit, that had for years been considered as not much more than a pest, now became a life saver for many villagers and turned up on the table in every conceivable form. Rabbit Pie, hot or cold, stewed with dumplings and many more. Most households had a chicken run and when the occupants were in the mood, the lid on the powdered egg tin could stay put, but this, together with Spam, were the two most disliked products to cross our shores. For the wives and mothers eking out the meagre rations, it must have been a nightmare and what to use as sandwich fillings tested the imagination to the nth degree. One of our workmen used to turn up with a mixture of semolina and beetroot in his sandwiches, not much to work on, but he is still alive and kicking today.

The German bombers seemed to prefer the dark winter nights to be a nuisance and stooged around quite low, dropping the odd bombs here and there. The cock pheasants nearest to the explosion gave their "Cock-up" warning cry, which was repeated by the next nearest and so on until the sound faded in the distance. In the autumn of '41, a ju 87 (dive-bomber) was damaged over Peterborough and heading south crossed St. Neots on fire before crashing at Colmworth. Everyone from Hail Weston to Croxton said, "It passed right over my house", a nice one to tell the grandchildren.

This was the nearest enemy plane to be brought down around here although a couple of Flying Bombs reached as far as Eaton Socon. Late one afternoon in November '42 a local farmer had a shock, as out of the mist, a German plane emerged at tree-top height, minutes before it had attacked Lt. Barford Power station and was on its way to find another target but was brought down by a Spitfire in Wellingborough.

Quite a few of our own bombers made unscheduled returns to earth, among which were an RAF bomber that crashed at Melchbourne, a fighter that came down only the distance of a six-hit from Kimbolton Grammar School and a Mosquito from Lt.Staughton airfield, which developed engine failure when setting off on a raid, was blown to pieces by its own bombs. When the Americans arrived with their B17's – the complicated formation flying they were trying to perfect, coupled with the unpredictable English weather, caused all sorts of problems and deserves a separate story.

A wonderful community spirit helped to keep up morale and Winston Churchill's stirring speeches made everyone feel part of the War Effort. The Royal Family played their part by continuing to live in London and regularly visited the worst of the blitzed areas, as well as factories and operational airfields.

When the end of the War came in 1945 the VE celebrations released six years of pent up emotions and were held throughout the land. But for those whose loved ones did not return life would never be the same again.

Wartime Memories

This part of the East Midlands, with its gently undulating terrain, provided the ideal location for siting a good number of the airfields needed for operations in WW11. The prime requirements for an airbase would be a plateau of land of at least one square mile that was not crossed by a main road or a water course and few inhabitants. Within a radius of about eighteen miles of Kimbolton there were some twenty airfields constructed and from 1942 onwards the sight or sound of aircraft overhead was almost continuous and during the night, not always of the friendly variety. About half of these airfields were for the American Air Force that operated by day and the rest of the airfields were occupied by the RAF and they did the night shift. For obvious reasons, the planes that were going on missions had their engines warmed up well in advance and when the Americans were preparing for one of their long distance strikes it meant that at around 4am the noise, mid-way between Kimbolton and Thurleigh (which is where we lived) of up to 160 planes x 1200 hp engines flat out, was indescribable, whichever way the wind was blowing. A huge number of ground staff was needed to keep the show on the road and many of the big country mansions were commandeered for various activities.

Lilford Hall was turned into a massive hospital for American casualties and Gaynes Hall for training the special agents that were parachuted into Europe from Tempsford 'drome. Melchbourne Park was the headquarters of the American Air Force and an auditorium was built there for Glen Miller and his boys to practise their spellbinding dance music. Some distance away, a large wooded area was honeycombed with concrete roads for a bomb storage depot, the bombs being delivered to Kimbolton Railway Station and ferried to and fro by what seemed like a team of Formula One drivers! Local traffic soon decided that discretion was the better part of valour and pulled over when one of these convoys came into view. The main reason why the 'George Corner' remained intact was because at that time it was the best pub in the area and so popular with the American top brass, it's a wonder that they did not put it under armed guard. Not only did The George have a convivial bar and lounge, the dining room was also well appointed and "mine host", at that time was young, female, attractive and single. What more could a service man want 3000 miles from home?

After the landlady left in 1952 the business went into decline, mainly due to the Brewers selecting unsuitable tenants and the pub was finally sold off for housing. What a shame, but then nothing stays the same for ever and in any case, "time, like an ever rolling stream, bears all its sons (and daughters) away."

When the Yanks came Marching In

After the Americans had belatedly entered the war at the beginning of 1941 a decision was made by the Allies to knock Germany out and then turn their attention onto Japan. Before any invasion of the continent could be considered, the softening up process, involved England being virtually turned into an island aircraft carrier.

The huge factories in the USA could turn out over a hundred bombers per week and the crews could be trained in the Mid West, under perfect weather conditions.

The basic plan was centred round the 'B'17's or Flying Fortresses being manoeuvred into what was known as a box formation. Three layers of planes flying at a height above the range of anti-aircraft fire and sufficient .5 machine guns to cover all angles of attack. This had worked well in training, but over here in the fog, mist, low cloud and frequent changes in wind direction an average of one plane was lost per day by collisions alone. The German ack ack fire had been upgraded so that it could reach however high the allied planes flew and the German fighters later in the war were equipped with cannons so they could pop off at the Yanks, while sitting out of range of their .5 machine guns. Sending these formations deep into Germany without fighter protection was akin to the Romans putting the Christians in with the lions in the Coliseum.

The B17 which made several passes over Kimbolton Castle at a recent anniversary celebration rekindled the memories and made the hair stand up on the back of our necks. Someone had done a good job and everyone appreciated the effort, but this was like comparing chalk with cheese to what went on during the war. These monsters would take off at dawn so heavily laden with fuel and bombs according to the task ahead, with every single one of their five thousand horsepower straining within the metal frame to get it airborne and into formation before disappearing into the distance.

Later they were to return, often as stragglers, some with one engine not working and the lucky ones with two but with lumps missing from wings and the carnage inside left to the imagination. On some missions 30% were lost. Kimbolton lost six out of 18 on the raid to the ball bearing factory at Sweinfurt, sixty young chaps each one some parents' son.

They were well looked after by their government, smart uniforms plenty of cigarettes, chocolate, chewing gum and it is said nylons. I don't know if they were for them to wear or help with various negotiations. They also knew how to enjoy themselves especially at the dances where they would spin the girls round at such speed that their skirts stood out like windsocks in a gale and when the jitter bug music started the girls were flying around like rag dolls. Mind you they went mainly for the lightweight girls but with rationing there were plenty of slim line models on offer.

It is difficult to find a word to describe the mood of people around at that time. Probably resignation might be the one because destiny was not in our own hands. We were dependant on others and if the American boys were willing to risk their lives daily to save ours and fancied a fling with a local girl, no one would really give a damn. There were far more important things to worry about.

Many were the stories that were floating around at that time and I like the story from Pertenhall School where the mistress encouraged the pupils to listen to the wireless and read the papers to broaden their education. After prayers she would ask for any news from the war. One young boy whose father was away in the RAF put his hand up and said, "Please miss, we had an American come for supper last night and he stayed for breakfast". As the saying goes, 'some are lucky and some are not'.

The Last Chance Saloon

Towards the end of the depression that had lasted from 1921-39 much of the heavy arable land in this area had been uneconomic to crop and was left to return to nature.

As the war got underway the U Boats started to play havoc with the merchant shipping so starvation began to loom large and in early 1943 the country had only 6 weeks food supply left. When the threat of invasion ended thousands of Italian prisoners who had been captured in the North African campaign were brought over here to work on the farms, helping to bring the derelict land back into production. Camps were set up around the country and our local one was Ducks Cross at Colmworth. A group of about a dozen prisoners, complete with an armed guard were hedging and ditching at Tilbrook between the main road and the Kimbolton Estate.

During the afternoon of Friday 9th July 1943 one of the prisoners who at his inquest a week later was described as becoming "mentally unstable" complained that his hedging hook needed sharpening and was taken back to the rest hut to do the necessary but when the guard's back was turned the prisoner killed him with a single blow of the hook. The assailant then made off towards the woods with the loaded rifle and some Land Girls hoeing sugar beet in an adjoining field who tried to stop him were fired at, but fortunately off target.

The police and army decided against putting a search party into the woods as further loss of life would probably ensue and it was hoped that he would surrender. The Home Guard set up road-blocks around the area to contain him and any residents within the cordon were advised to remain vigilant.

Scene two of the drama took place the next day a mile to the south of where the guard lost his life in an isolated farmhouse at Pertenhall. Sid Shelton and his son John had just finished tea, John opened the kitchen door into the hall to go to feed the hens, when, there in front of him stood the prisoner who fired a shot at John at point blank range, which somehow missed.

The prisoner then ran up the front stairs and John grabbed his Home Guard rifle and went up the back stairs. A game of cat and mouse then ensued where, as Ann Robinson points out, there can only be one winner. John, knowing the lie of the land managed to get the first shot in on target and the man-hunt was over.

For his act of extreme bravery John was awarded the BEM by King George VI at Buckingham Palace. At a subsequent interview John played down his part and said he was lucky to be alive himself. His good fortune he said was that the prisoner had entered the house through the pantry window, drank a jug of milk and ate two harvest pies. One would give you indigestion and two would probably induce double vision and the prisoner shot at "the wrong one".

John and I have been good friends all our lives and were together at KGS from "36 – 41". He was always in the top three in class and his only black mark being late nearly every morning – the excuse because he had to let the hens out before setting off on his bike. On July 10 1943 they were late getting fed in the afternoon.

COUNTY OF BEDFORD.
CIVIL DEFENCE.
1939 — 1945.

CLAUDE HENRY CHARLES BANKS, WARDEN'S SERVICE, PERTENHALL.

The County Council through their Emergency Committee desire, on the disbanding of the Civil Defence General Services, to thank you for the unstinted and valuable service you have rendered as a member of the Organisation.

Your loyalty and devotion to duty, particularly during the time when this Country suffered most heavily, contributed in no small measure to the safety of your fellow citizens and to keeping high the morale of the Nation.

The Service has throughout justified to the full the confidence which has been placed in it, and you may be justly proud of the part you played in a task so well accomplished.

Chairman, Bedfordshire County Council
and of the County Emergency Committee.

Clerk of the County Council
and County Controller.

2nd May, 1945.

Scanned document of Claude's County of Bedford civil defence certificate

An Epic Act of Chivalry

Fighting has been going on ever since man evolved many hundreds of thousands of years ago when tribes competed for hunting grounds and fertile areas of land for growing crops. Friendly tribes joined forces to repel invaders such as the Vikings who crossed the North Sea from Scandinavia to enjoy a spot of raping and pillaging along our east coast. The leaders of these tribes became kings who led their armies into battle and some like King Harold were mortally wounded in the conflict. Countries now ruled by politicians, are unable or unwilling to curb the invasion of immigrants, illegal or otherwise, send our troops to fight other people in far off lands. One might excuse them if they led their troops into action, like the Kings of long ago, then I suspect that very soon wars would be fewer and farther between.

The scene was set for this story on December 20th 1943 when an attack on the F.W. Plant at Bremen by the American Air Force that included a squad of B17's from the Kimbolton Airbase. Details have been gleaned from various sources including "Contrails" the 379 Squadron's regular magazine. One of the planes named "Ye Old Pub" was piloted by 2nd Lt Charles Brown and was severely damaged by flak on the bomb run. The nose section was completely smashed as well as two of the engines and some of the controls to a lesser extent which resulted in the plane losing its place in the formation and was isolated from the squadron, then 15 ME109's set upon it in a battle that lasted a quarter of an hour during which time it shot down one enemy plane and damaged several others. Four crew members were badly wounded and the action only stopped when the plane spiralled down out of control from 25000 feet, during which time due to the cold of –60c and lack of oxygen all the crew had lost consciousness. Brown remembers coming round in time to level out just above tree top height and head off in the general direction of home. They were in a sorry state and a sitting target for any enemy that wanted to add one more to his total. To their horror one such appeared flying along side of them and a penny for their thoughts at that time would have represented poor value as to their chances of seeing home again.

However, the German pilot, an old hand as further events were to reveal, quickly summed up the situation and could see through the windows and holes in the fuselage crew members attending to their wounded comrades and were no threat to him. Various hand signals between the two pilots resulted in the B17 being escorted out over the North Sea and eventually to land at Seething a base near the coast in Norfolk. The German pilot reported the B17 as crashing in the sea, any other outcome would have seen him severely disciplined or even made to pay the ultimate price for letting an enemy plane escape. After all is said and done the Americans had been dishing out a lot of stick for well over a year and for many a Fritz and Fraulein the GI's were certainly not first choice flavour of the month.

During 1986 Charles Brown initiated a search with whoever could help locate the pilot who so gallantly had shown mercy to a helpless foe. In 1990 Franny Steigler identified himself and was actually living in Canada, only 200 miles from Brown's home. A big reunion party was organised that lasted for three days and notes were compared. Steigler had accounted for 28 allied planes. He had been wounded four times, shot down 17 times, nine of which by bomber gunners. Stories such as this restore our faith in humanity and a favourite quote neatly rounds it up.

"When the one great scorer comes to write against our name, he'll ask not if we lost or won, but how we played the game". Franny Steigler certainly knew how to.

Jack the Lad
(Jack Boatman) 1921-2014

Sniffing out a good story is the easy part, getting the detail is more difficult as in this case, the health of my quarry had for some time been so poorly that on a couple of occasions he had been within touching distance of the Pearly Gates but before St. Peter could let him in modern technology shepherded him back into the fold. Secondly, squeezing it into the available space is more like getting a litre into a liqueur glass than a quart into a pint pot.

Jack's family came to Hargrave in the mid 1930's when his father, who was an agent for a hay and straw merchant, was allocated this part of the East Midlands and was provided with the first telephone in the village. This became handy for the locals to use and also for the Home Guard, which had been formed in 1940 to combat the expected invasion.

He was enlisted into the Royal Navy in 1943 after several interviews where the powers that be did their damndest to get him into the Army, but his strength of character pulled him through. Not for him, life in the floating barracks, that was the nickname for battleships, but the daredevil existence with service in a squadron of MTB's.★ These small craft with a crew of about ten operated from ports along the south coast to harry the German shipping on the other side of the channel. Their main armament was a torpedo tube either side and a front mounted six pounder gun which was proving more miss that hit in skirmishes against the German E Boats with their crack 88 mm weapons. Jack quickly worked out the modifications that were necessary and when implemented left the flotilla in better shape.

By this time the family had moved to Stow Longa and when on leave Jack became friendly with the American Airmen, so much so, he was taken up in practice flights and on one occasion acted as a crew member in a B17 flying Fortress on a raid on Cologne. Luckily they were not attacked by enemy fighters but were peppered with AA fire.

Returning from leave his CO asked him if he had done anything interesting while away and when told about the Cologne trip he wondered who should be saluting who.

On demob Jack joined forces with Bill Hellett another ex. Serviceman and formed a haulage company that is still going strong today. One of their first jobs was to construct a road from the end of Hatchet Lane to our buildings at College Farm with hardcore from demolitions at the airfield.

He has been one of the leading lights in the local branch of the British Legion and for many years had the honour on Remembrance Sunday reading the names of those who, in the two World Wars, had given their tomorrow so that we could have our today.

* Motor Torpedo Boats

From Negligence to Negligee

Salisbury Plain has always been the recognised area set-aside for Army manoeuvres, whilst leafy shire villages were left to do their own thing, mainly to feed the nation and for old folk to expound at great length, with the benefit of hindsight, why things are not as good as they used to be, but according to our grandparents, they never were.

Early one morning about mid-May 1944 to say we had the shock of our lives would be putting it mildly. When we went out to work we found our farm-yard had been taken over by part of an armoured division that had spread itself over Kimbolton and the surrounding villages. The most likely reason for the selection of this area was its similarity to the part of Brittany our troops would encounter after moving off the D-Day beachheads, namely narrow roads and small fields crossed by streams with bridges and wooded areas to negotiate. All this did not help our morning routine of feeding the livestock and milking before moving on later to arable tasks. Soldiers were in most of the barns cooking their breakfast on primus stoves amongst the hay and straw, a disaster waiting to happen.

The overnight plan for me to be working on a tractor at the Swineshead end of the farm and Dad and the rest of the gang to be at the Stonely end was allowed to stand but about midday the sight of one of our farm worker's wives waving frantically at the top end of the field was the last thing I wanted to see. "The soldiers have set the farm on fire and you had better take my bike". The hundreds of times I had ridden that road on my school bike did not prepare me for action on her 'sit up and beg' high stepper. These bikes had always been constructed more for maiden aunts than for someone to get from A to B in less time than an Olympic cyclist on a time trial. The fire had been going for sometime and in a stack of wheat, thankfully not in the farm buildings. The Army had scarpered and the local fire engine and crew were doing their stuff. Putting out a fire in a corn stack cannot be achieved by just pouring water on as it just keeps smouldering away and had to be dismantled sheaf by sheaf. The stack was the produce of about a dozen acres and how to spread it about in the confines of a rick yard, by then ankle deep in mud and water, could not have been found in any manual entitled 'How to become a successful Farmer'. Apparently as soon as the order came to 'stand down' the Tommies threw fire crackers up in celebration and one landed on the stack.

Life is one long learning curve which for some of those young men would soon be coming to an end. War is a nasty business and the Hippies slogan 'make love not war' the more enjoyable of the two alternatives. Everyone had a tale to tell of the damage caused locally especially of the livestock that had to be rounded up afterwards. Tank drivers do not open gates, they just drive over them. Two tanks had driven skew across Kimbolton cricket-square and it took several decades before the track marks could be eradicated.

Without the benefit of the three main services, electricity, water and sewerage, life in the villages was far more spartan than today and every household had a daily routine to suit. On one Swineshead farm it was the wife who kick-started proceedings by going downstairs to put a match to the fire that had been laid overnight before taking herself back upstairs to get dressed. That morning the dog was barking so still half asleep she went downstairs to let it out before it woke the neighbours and found herself amongst a group of soldiers cooking their breakfast under the apple tree. This would have been a knock out for Candid Camera but for the Army boys Christmas had come early. For the lady it must have been heart stopping. Night-dresses come in all shapes and sizes but are not the usual attire for strolling around the garden at 6 o'clock in the morning. To be fair this was not her worst wartime experience as a couple of years earlier a telegram had arrived with news that her son had been killed in action.

Those of us who seem to enjoy looking for things to grumble about might be better served counting our blessings.

Stranger on the Shore

This was the signature tune that Acker Bilk's Jazz Band used to captivate the hearts and minds of music lovers in the 1960's. Other strangers have left their footprints in the sands of history, especially in the mid 1930's when a rumour spread around the villages that a "black man" was working in Bedford. At that time the National Bus Company ran shopping trips to Bedford from Kimbolton each Saturday and this usually attracted about a dozen customers. When the news broke of a foreign gentleman in town the bus was full before it reached Ravensden. How many people were lucky enough to catch sight of him I don't know, but he became one of the bus drivers and turned out to be a really popular guy,

The war brought many immigrants to our shores, the first were known as 'displaced persons' and camps were set up to house them. Three Latvians worked for the Anglia River Board cutting out the undergrowth in the brooks in front of the dragline with axes and trimming hooks, no chainsaw in those days and these chaps would have held their own in any company, as far as work was concerned. By the end of 1941 the Italian prisoners had started to arrive and soon exploded the myth that Italian men were lazy and sat around smoking, while their women folk did the work. The ones that were detailed to our farm were conscientious, honest and good company and although we pulled their legs about what their wives might be up to whilst they were away, they took no offence and no more wanted the war than we did. When they were repatriated in 1945, German prisoners took their place and were a different kettle of fish. A good many were sullen, arrogant and resentful, but others were pretty decent chaps and a few stayed on to marry English girls and integrated into society.

The Commonwealth countries sent a generation of their youth over to help the Motherland in its hour of need, the Canadians being the nearest, when they occupied the Pathfinder base at Lt.Gransden. At the end of the war, we were lucky enough to welcome Canadian Ground crew Harry Broughton into our family, when he married one of my sisters.

Harry and a dozen of his mates were farm hands on the prairies when they volunteered, but during training my brother-in-law developed air-sickness and was relegated to ground staff duties. This no doubt saved his life, as none of his mates survived to return to their farms and families.

At the time of writing, Harry is now 96 and my sister Stancie 92 and they will, God willing, soon celebrate their 70th Wedding anniversary, where they settled in Vancouver, Canada.

Back to the story – the Americans, who for three years dominated the area, deserved better than to be labelled, "overpaid, over sexed and over here". If their government considered that they were worth that wage, that was up to them. If they were over sexed, it was presumably bred in them and not many leopards have been known to change their spots and lastly it is a good thing they were over here, because had they not been, the war would not have been won by the Allies.

The American's dislikes were understandable.

The weather – they claimed it was the main reason that we had not been invaded since 1066.

The mud – our boulder clay that is responsible for the success of farming in this area, when wet and paddled about on quickly resembles that product which sticks to blankets.

Brussel Sprouts – one pilot, out of fuel, pancaked his plane in a field of potatoes and was admonished by his commanding officer for not ditching in a field of sprouts.

The American likes were:

Driving large vehicles very fast and usually on the wrong side of the road.

Playing Poker and Blackjack for very high stakes.

Anything in a skirt (but not necessarily in that order).

The Grafton Underwood base was high on the list of USAF achievements. It was the first to be occupied and the first and last to drop bombs on Germany. History may yet add another first, because a couple of days after arrival, the Commanding Officer decided to send a couple of truck loads of G.I's down into Thrapston to meet the locals, make a good impression and, like Cinderella, be home before midnight. He obviously neglected to tell them to bring all their equipment back with them, as the next morning, the park keeper, tidying up, found an American gas mask and an item of ladies underwear in close proximity. Whilst it is unwise to arrive at hasty conclusions, two and two occasionally add up to four!

CHAPTER SIX

Weather

The Storm, August, 2nd 1906

Readers will have noted Claude's fascination with the weather and in particular extremes of weather as the world seems to be suffering at present. Here follow two accounts of the Storm on August, 2nd 1906.

Many and varied will be the accounts given in years to come but to ensure a true and uncoloured version being preserved, I write this. J.R.Newman, County Councillor for Middlesex 06.08.1906

"It had been a hot day with the sun beating down from a cloudless sky, then about 7.30pm away in the west black clouds were rising with lightening signalling the approaching storm. Half an hour later a breeze sprang up, the lightening increased and thunder began to roll and everyone made for home.

I was staying at the Post Office in the centre of the village of Lt.Staughton and the experience I had is a reflection of what all who were in the track of the storm had to cope with.

About 8.30pm I stood out in the roadway and the lightening became continuous. First one part of the sky and then another was lit up in a dazzling manner and the thunder was so deafening, I decided to go indoors for safety, where I found neighbours had congregated to comfort one another. Just before the hail started at about 9 o'clock the wind force had increased and tore through the trees like a blast from a furnace. Words fail to describe the events of the next 20 minutes. A tremendous roar was heard, followed by hailstones as big as walnuts or bigger and being driven by the gale descended like an avalanche of bullets. Bang, crash the window blind was billowing in like a balloon showing the panes of glass were shattered. I tried to hold it in place but was forced to retreat farther into the house. It seemed as if the end of the world had come, but soon the hail stopped the wind dropped and we were to survey the damage. The house was flooded and opening the door facing the road the hailstones were piled up to a foot deep and on the road, a level of 4 to 5 inches, mixed with leaves and fruit stripped from the trees.

About 10 o'clock the storm had passed and the light of the full moon glistened on the ice in the fields around and a scene of grandeur now appeared in the shape of a magnificent rainbow that spread from Hill Farm gateway to Gt.Staughton. The highest part of the arc was above the church, that sadly dawn would reveal, had 165 broken panes of glass"

This is an abbreviated account, as space does not allow for the full coverage. One wonders how some of the inhabitants coped in the aftermath as those with bedrooms facing the storm would have had soaked beds covered in glass that would take days to dry out, as well as the thought of the ruined crops. However they had been bred and brought up to withstand adversity and at least no lives had been lost.

Every so often nature demonstrates its unlimited power, as if to remind us that man is not always the boss however important some world leaders might imagine themselves to be.

A Phenomenal Storm
(From Claude's Research)

August 2nd 1906 – the most devastating storm to vent it's fury on this part of the country, since records began in 1650.

According to official reports the storm brewed up in the East Midlands in the early evening and travelled in a north-easterly direction, snaking its way across East Anglia and out into The Wash. One correspondent compared it to a "Thunderstorm of Biblical intensity". As it reached Woburn it was accompanied by gale force winds and torrential hail that smashed and flattened the ripening crops and broke most of the windows in the side of houses exposed to its force. The hailstorm itself lasted about 20 minutes and varied from one to two miles wide. This was of no consolation to those in its path who had their harvest and livelihood ruined. Had it not been for many local benefactors and a nation wide appeal by the Daily Telegraph hundreds of farmers, small holders and farm workers would have faced an uncertain future as to feeding their families and livestock and paying their bills without any income from their cereal crops.

The storm carried on from Moulsoe, via Astwood, Stagsden and Harrold, with some fields on the fringe half ruined and the other half barely touched. In Oakley and Milton Ernest numerous trees were uprooted and gangs of men worked through the night to clear the main A6 road. On it went through Thurleigh followed by Bolnhurst where 60 rabbits were found dead the next morning killed by the hail stones that resembled lumps of ice, many measuring more than five inches in circumference and were still lying around in drifts 24 hours later. The Bedfordshire Times reported that Keysoe Row, a densely populated area by rural standards, was badly affected and named a dozen farmers and small holders who had seen their harvest wiped out before their very eyes.

Little Staughton also lay in the storm's path and the inhabitants would have been forgiven for thinking that there were hidden forces at work in retribution for some previous misdemeanour as only six years before their beautiful church had been struck by lightening and the top 15 feet of the spire was still surrounded by the repair scaffolding. A number of plovers and several coveys of partridge in an adjacent field paid the ultimate price for being in the wrong place at the wrong time. Further on the storm crossed the B645, just east of the fireworks factory and did great damage to the crops on Claylands, Priory and Lymage Farms, on its way through Easton, Ellington, Alconbury, Ramsey Heights and Pondersbridge.

During earlier times, long before the "Global warming" scares had been invented by politicians to take the public's mind off the really important things that are going wrong, hailstones were much more frequent than in modern times and most farmers insured their

Claude with Swans on farm reservoir

cereal crops. However, when the North American Prairies were opened up in the mid 1800's, cheap wheat flooded Western Europe and farming went into steep decline. Savings had to be made and expensive insurance policies were the first to go, but as we all know, it is easy to be wise after the event.

Sunny Side Up

The subject of the weather is a good conversation opener and in this area during unsettled periods most people have a different tale to tell. Fifty years ago before Grafham Water was constructed Brampton was reckoned to be one of the driest villages in the country, but that is not the case today. Apparently the area of water at Grafham is large enough to cool the air above it and causes precipitation which then descends on Brampton.

The meteorological office puts together the forecasts, which we as farmers listen to with great concern, are lucky if they get it more than 50% right, with Michael Fish having egg on his face in September 1987 over the gale that wrecked most of southern England. On the evening in question, just on dusk, our old cock pheasant who had roosted for a couple of years in the cherry tree in our garden at Stonely decided to have the night sitting on a honeysuckle bush trellised on the North East wall of our farm house. We thought he was suffering from an early onset of senile dementia but he knew more than Michael Fish and had he taken notice of his forecast he would have woken up the next morning half way to Easton.

Many years ago an old guy from Souldrop wrote articles for the Bedfordshire Times, a weekly publication that had a wide circulation covering most of the county and beyond. His theme was mainly weather related and every year around October time he forecast we would have a white Christmas. When it eventually happened he became famous and reporters from the National Press descended on Souldrop to interview their home grown clairvoyant.

One of the good things about the weather is that it treats us all the same; old or young, rich or poor and we can do nothing about it, so we should all count our blessings and try to be positive.

My experience, for what it is worth, in this area our weather seems to go in ten to fourteen day cycles and then changes, so saying the weather tomorrow would be much the same as today would be right more times than it was wrong.

In 1956 we finished harvest on October 22nd and in 1976 we finished on July 31st so the only thing predicable about the weather is its unpredictability.

A Rum Old Time

The favourable weather experienced for the wartime harvests went a long way towards our ability to withstand the blockade by the U-boats that threatened our food supplies. It was equally important that the fine spells continued through the autumns to enable the valuable root crops to be brought in and the winter seed sown, which is the backbone of the next year's harvest.

There is no doubt in my mind that if there is such a thing as divine intervention, we were the beneficiaries at that time because the following harvest in 1946 was the wettest ever and many crops were left in the field. No improvement came until April '47 as the autumn was a washout with almost no seed sown and during December severe frost made life on the farm difficult, with water supplies for the livestock having to be continuously thawed and cars' and tractors' cooling systems drained overnight. There was no anti-freeze in those days. Christmas came and went in a blur and always with a worry of what could go wrong next. Not many voices could be heard proclaiming the joy of "being a farmer's boy".

January 1947 certainly did bring the snow, about a foot of it and blizzard conditions left drifts 15 feet deep in places and traffic ground to a halt. All farm workers who were not otherwise involved with livestock welfare, were taken on by the County Councils and given shovels to clear the drifts, as mechanical diggers were not available at the time. Dairy farmers were at their wits end – where to store the milk that the lorry could not get round to collect. We had milk in every available container, including the family bath. Tradesmen could not deliver and had it not been for Les James, a Stow Longa farmer, who had bought a Bren Gun Carrier at an Army disposal sale, coming round with bread, groceries and meat, many villagers would have gone hungry. He also conveyed a coffin to a funeral, as the hearse was snowbound.

During February and March, high pressure set in and warm afternoons melted a little of the snow that had frozen solid at night and soon everywhere was covered in ice, several inches thick, with rabbits and hares having to climb trees and eat the bark to survive.

The change came on March 26th, with the wind switching from NE to SW and the temperature from minus too plus. Within 24 hours, most of the ice and snow had melted, but, with the ground still frozen, the water ran off the top and into the water courses and floods appeared, sweeping away all of the wooden footbridges. For several days, St. Neots resembled Venice. The Fens were inundated and life for many became very fraught and the old saying that "fire and water are good servants, but bad masters" had more than a ring of truth about it.

Football fixtures were so far in arrears, that in April we were playing two midweek evening fixtures and on the last Saturday of the season, one game in the afternoon and another in the evening, followed by a trip to the pub and on to the Mandeville Hall for the dance. We had to make our own amusement in those days and playing sport enabled us to make many friends. It kept us fit and with contented minds.

One of those days that did not end as well as it began

The morning of Sunday, 20th May, 1950 gave no indication anything untoward was likely to happen. The weather was fine and sunny and for the farming community, the crops were looking well. A period of slack time was coming up, to enable farmers to prepare for the hay time and harvest ahead and find time to stick pins in effigies of the Agriculture Minister, John Strachey, who had recently said that the new subsidy system had made farmers feather-bedded.

During a lunchtime drink at the now defunct pub, 'The Kangaroo', three of us decided to have an afternoon at the farm at Stonely shooting a few pigeons. This was proving quite successful, but a storm brewing up to the south west prompted one of the guests to suggest we packed up, this turned out to be a wise move as soon after we got home torrential rain fell, the like of which had never been seen before nor since in this area and in less than an hour over four inches (100mm) was recorded.

About 6.30pm, the pop-pop sound of our upstream neighbour's

Field Marshall tractor alerted us that a flood was on its way and we set about bringing to safety, a couple of hundred chicks that were in brooders, close to the brook and in the few minutes it took us to do that, we were almost swept off our feet by the rising water. The only dry place on the farmstead was in one of the spare bedrooms and newspaper was laid on the floor for the chick's new home. By this time the house was surrounded by water and over a foot deep inside, so we retired upstairs to survey the muddy water rushing by and were amazed to see, on the flood, a bale of straw with a Rhode Island Red hen, perched precariously on the top. "Look Dad", I said "at that poor hen". He replied, "That ought to be Bloody Strachey".

A mile away a small stream that collected water from not much more than a couple of square miles had flooded the Swineshead road and a petrol Land Rover vehicle driven by a mother with small son and daughter on board had stalled, bang in the middle of the stream. The mother was faced with making a quick decision, to try and take the boy to dry land and come back for the girl. As soon as she and the boy tried to wade to safety they were swept off their feet. Had it not been for John Shelton and his sister Sheila being on hand, as they were saving their poultry, coming to the rescue of the stricken people in the water, the mother and her son would almost certainly have lost their lives. In the few minutes it took before they could turn their attention to the plight of the girl, the land rover was swallowed up into the bed of the stream and the little girl sadly drowned. To illustrate the strength and depth of the flood a number of felled trees each weighing several tons and awaiting collection were carried over the road by the rushing water and deposited on a manure heap in an adjoining field.

This is another example of tragedy, caused by a freak of nature, made worse by the victim being so young and a combination of circumstances that is unlikely to occur again. This tiny area of Bedfordshire about the size of half a dozen football pitches has seen more than its fair share of disturbing events, including being the first place in the county where German bombs dropped in October

1939. In early May 1943, the Pertenhall valley was used on moonlit nights, for practice runs by the Dambusters. One plane was flying so low, that it took 15 feet off the top of the elm tree adjacent to the bridge, where the disaster of the flood took place and the plane was more than lucky to stay airborne. These stories, along with the saga of the Italian prisoner (see The Last Chance Saloon), gives the locals plenty of tales to tell their grandchildren.

John Shelton BEM 1925-2014

Shades of the B17s

As I write this article World leaders are meeting to discuss methods of halting climate change but considering it has been going on for millions of years before man even evolved, any tangible success will be limited.

Everything seems to revolve around the amount of CO^2 being produced and even scientists cannot agree on what can or should be done about it, some accused of massaging figures to get the result they need which smacks of the old "weapons of mass destruction" sound bite that led us up the garden path to the Iraq war.

Our Government has mismanaged the economy and run up debts that our grandchildren will still be paying off and are beating the climate change drum to take our minds from the wolf at our door and if covering the landscape with wind turbines is the best they can come up with, they are naive as well as deceitful and dishonest.

I would like to add some of my experiences to the climate change debate.

When I was a boy, windmills were common place and I often went, with one of Grandfather's men, to deliver grain to be ground for stock feed, to the windmill at Keysoe. Had they been that efficient, why were they allowed to fall into disrepair?

Fifty years ago, Thurleigh was one of three sites surveyed for the third London airport but was turned down because it was fog prone. Reading reports of the 379th Bomb Group at Kimbolton reveals the number of days they were "fogged in". Wind disperses fog so this area is definitely unsuitable.

Politicians will say anything true or false that increases their chance of re-election and are therefore conveniently steering clear of the most obvious problem which is the population explosion that will run the world short of food in another century and without CO^2 life on earth could not have evolved. We were taught at school that the green colouring matter in plants (chlorophyll) enables them to take in CO_2, use the carbon for growth and expel oxygen for us to breath. No crop growing land should be built upon, use brown field sites, and any waste land should be planted with trees to help clean the air.

Our Prime Minister should stop giving our money away to make him look big on the world stage. We are a small country and charity should begin at home. His moral compass has led us down a dead end and prudence no longer resides at No.10, but all is not doom and gloom. About four years ago a mobile phone company wanted to erect a mast alongside our grain barn at Stonely but planning consent would be needed from the local council. This was denied because it would spoil a site of outstanding beauty (that was a new one on me). So we can rest assured that the Kimbolton Parish Council will veto the Bicton Wind Farm being just the same distance from St. Andrews Church as our grain barn.

P.S. No prizes are available for revealing its new site!!!

A Winter to Remember

As I write this a few days before Christmas 2010 we are experiencing some very uncomfortable wintry weather but we all know that predicting what the future holds is a very dodgy business, as those experts from the Met Office who forecast a mild winter are well aware.

I'm sure soon the situation may be far different with perhaps snowdrops and crocuses resplendent in our gardens, or God forbid, a repeat of 1962/63. Up to now the similarities are beginning to stack up, snow before the end of November and record low temperatures through December that have caught out any water pipes that were not well insulated. Back then many houses were without water, the underground mains having frozen up. We at College Farm were among the unlucky ones and although being without water for a day is very inconvenient, to be denied for several weeks one has to draw on hidden reserves that have built up in the DNA of those whose ancestors have survived trial and tribulation to wrest a living from the unforgiving soil.

I was fortunate that Daphne was equally resilient. She melted snow in saucepans on the AGA to flush the toilets and with three nippers under the age of seven to cater for, as well as a husband, whose mood was often similar to he who has lost a half crown and found a shilling. Light relief came twice a week when we took the children to friends and relatives for baths. We were welcomed into their homes with open arms. A friend in need is a friend indeed.

The winter of 46/47 was equally harsh and lasted much longer but more than a foot of snow insulated the ground and subterraneous water pipes escaped Jack Frost. Our main problem then was thawing out the drinking tanks for our livestock, horses, cattle, sheep, pigs, hens and geese but by 62/63 these had all gone in an effort to keep ahead of the game of earning a living and providing funds for an annual holiday at Clacton. Recently I found a bill from that era "The Hadleigh Hotel" One week's full board for two adults, three children, morning tea and papers plus car parking £115-10s-6d. We had great fun on the beach with sand castles and Punch and Judy show, which beats sitting in an airport lounge waiting for a plane to Costa-del-somewhere.

By 62/63 we had included Brussels sprouts, potatoes and sugar beet into our crop rotation, which brought a problem of a different kind. Every pigeon in Europe flew across the North Sea to attack the sprouts in East Anglia. They had to eat a vast amount to combat the cold and provide energy to fly and were soon almost sitting targets for those who had enough time and money to buy the cartridges. They were only skin, bone and feathers and worthless to sell.

We thought, come the thaw, we would be able to make good money from the remaining crop but a week after the thaw set in the stalks collapsed into a stinking morass and had to be ploughed in along with the dead pigeons.

Such was life on the farm at that time, and if you wake up one morning with the sun shining and everything in the garden looking lovely, cherish the moment, because tomorrow is another day.

Looking Ahead

As I write this at the end of May, we have had three consecutive months of drought and although an old saying goes, "A dry May and a dripping June sets everything in tune", is probably true, but this year it may well be too late.

Wild life is suffering especially the song bird population as the supply of caterpillars and flies to feed their young are not around owing to the adverse weather conditions. This is particularly galling for us as we are involved in one of the schemes that promote wild life habitats including spring sown crops that, as yet, have failed to germinate. Also a mile of new hedgerows planted during the winter was at risk with recent watering that has just disappeared down the cracks. It was said at one time, the two things never on view are a dead donkey and a happy farmer, but all we can do is try to work with nature and hope for the best and if a well known DIY store had stocked up on prayer mats instead of wellingtons they may not have gone up the Swanney.

The media keep reminding us of the recent driest years, particularly '59 and '76 but not a mention of 1921 which, according to what I was told as a boy, was the worst drought in living memory. The Chadwell Spring in Pertenhall was the only one that continued to flow and all the farmers from adjoining villages came with water carts to keep their animals alive. Branches from the elm trees were cut down for the cattle to eat the leaves and twigs with the straw from the winter barley crop devoured before autumn even arrived.

During the drought of '76 the weather experts said it would take two years of normal rainfall to fill the underground aquifers but on the August Bank Holiday Monday we had 2 inches which was the start of a wet autumn so bad that most of the winter wheat could not be drilled until December.

One of the latest crackpot schemes is a company trying to organise trips round the moon in a spacecraft but I would rather buy some shares in Noah's Ark Ltd.dot.com because the weather will average itself out and floods will appear at the least convenient time.

Now that they have reached maturity the two spinneys we planted in the autumn of '76 are providing warmth in winter and shade in summer and refuge for a host of wild life, which will still be around long after we are pushing up the daisies and a legacy for future generations to enjoy.

Claude with Swans on farm reservoir

CHAPTER SEVEN

Local Characters

The End of an Era

Before the days when horses were replaced by tractors it was not unusual for some of the farm workers to have spent their whole life on the same holding, many of them in tied cottages that went with the job. One would have been the horse keeper who more often than not was the foreman and in this case it was Herbert Saunders.

He lived and worked his whole life at West End Farm, Little Staughton, for three generations of the same family and towards the end of his 68 years his skill had become legendary. Nicknamed Wenney, he married Mary Briars a local girl who produced for him ten children, Archie, Charlie, Harold, Cliff, Bill, Eric, Joe, Elsie, Dorothy and Margery. As a boy he started working for our Grandfather who quickly spotted his potential and promoted him accordingly. His almost telepathic communication with his team of horses meant that reins were almost unnecessary and he always saw that the best oats, chaff and hay were kept for them.

Uncle Harry took over when Grandfather moved to Manor Farm, Pertenhall in 1917 but the link was maintained and Wenney was invited over on special occasions, one of them to help with the shearing which always took place on Derby Day. With about a couple of hundred sheep to cope with an extra pair of hands was welcome as electricity had not yet arrived so one man had to turn the handle while another wielded the clippers. Three of these sets were usually on the go with another man catching the sheep and getting them ready, whilst someone had the job of preparing the fleeces to be packed away in the wool sacks.

Henry Charles Banks, Claude's grandfather with
Dinky, his grand-daughter

One of Wenney's indulgencies was he liked to bet on the Derby and for all those prepared to listen were told he had backed the winner seven times out of the last ten years. What he did not tell them was he backed all horses whose names started with the letter 'S', any mounts owned by the Aga Khan and the one ridden by Gordon Richards so to bet 6d each way, he was mostly a loser and a winner at the same time.

Sunday lunch time was when he refuelled and later in life The Kangaroo was the port of call where he held court. Rats have always been a problem on farms and during the war a bounty of a shilling a dozen for their tails was an added incentive for their control. Wenney was a dab hand with his traps and every one he caught was the biggest B…y rat ever. One Sunday someone asked him how the size of the latest ones compared with those of long ago. After considerable thought he replied "Well Charlie, I think on average they are bigger now than they ever have been".

There is no doubt it was the end of an era when he passed away in 1952, his beloved cart horses had all but disappeared and now that on many farms the ploughs have been replaced by minimal cultivations one must start to wonder what will happen when the oil runs out.

Hot and Buttered

Nicknames were always part of the furniture as we grew up, some easy to work out, others less obvious.

The parents of John and Bob Westley ran a livery yard in Risely and one Saturday morning I was invited over to play, Bob being in a form below ours at KGS. As soon as I arrived, John's nickname of "Cub" manifested itself on the breeze because he had a pet fox in a kennel that had scratched a hole under the house foundations – the smell I will never forget.

Mr. Gibbard known as "Bant" probably from when he arrived in town, who was a bit on the stocky side, took great delight in looking behind some boys ears to see if they had washed.

At Dean the Hart boys were all good cricketers, the eldest Fred was known as "The Ace" and one Saturday he came as our umpire to Corby when we played Stuart and Lloyds.

Stan Leadbetter their star batsman had trials with Northants CC but that did not stop Fred giving him out LBW to a leg break. "That was never out" he exclaimed "Well look in the St Neots Advertiser next Thursday if you don't believe me" Fred replied. Corby was a rough place at that time and the stumps had to be taken into the pavilion at tea or they would get stolen.

Ken Hart, a younger brother, as a youth was quite slender and was given the handle of "Strib" after the featherweight boxer Stribling.

Albert (Bunny) Reynolds kept tame rabbits as a boy, each doe would have at least four litters a year and at about five a time, which he sold at Shaws Market and made a nice bit of pocket money to spend at yearly events like the Statty, the bus trip to Wicksteed Park and the weekly treat off Wrens Fish Van.

Robert Sharman and the Hunter twins, Gavin and James are about the only farmers around here who produce something to put between our slices of bread. The other thing they have in common is they were thrust into running their farms at an early age when both their fathers suffered fatal heart attacks.

Robert has in his genes the ability to deal in livestock inherited from his Grandfather "Hoogey" Sharman and I remember him coming to our place one day when I was about four years old to try to buy a litter of pigs. There seemed to be a big argument over the last shilling and when the deal looked like stalling he said "Well Charlie if you won't sell the pigs how much do you want for your little old boy?" A thousand pounds was mentioned, at which I bolted in the house and hid under the stairs, where I went whenever he turned up after that.

A few years ago Joe Bates had his Seventy Fifth birthday party at Squires Barn and after parking the car I walked up to the entrance where Joe was greeting his guests. To make a laugh I asked him if there would be any spare Crumpet around but before he could answer Robert's Mother, Dianne, a jolly good sport considering her unfortunate circumstances, had arrived and overheard the remark. She said "I am spare but unfortunately no longer Crumpet, now I qualify as a Muffin!" Just recently having suffered a broken ankle she gets around helping with the livestock on the ride-on lawn mower.

So now the old saying, "You can't keep a good man down" will have to include the Muffin as well.

PS. In 1930 £1,000 would have bought a 200 acre farm complete with house and buildings.

Bring me Sunshine

When William and Kate Cook came to farm at Pertenhall in 1912 with their four daughters and two sons, plus his brother always known as Uncle Tom, they would not have realised the beneficial impact two of them would have on the village in the years to come.

The youngest of the daughters, also named Kate, was only eighteen years of age when a vacancy came up at the Primary School for an infants' teacher and although not having had any training, Kate took it on and was very successful. I started at Pertenhall Primary School on my fourth birthday and under Miss Cook's care we sat on bench seats. We had slates, which were about 12 inches square and white chalk to write with and soon "The cat sat on the mat" was the first sentence put together.

Before the NHS came into being around 1950 life expectancy was far less than today and many families were to suffer fatalities that with modern medicines could be prevented. For the Cook family the loss of their eldest son William of pneumonia aged 21 in 1925 would have been a difficult cross to bear and his younger brother Jim, who had been sent to work as a rep for a local grain merchant, was brought back on to the farm to take his place.

By 1935 both parents had passed away and the farm had been left in equal shares between Jim and his four sisters. The two eldest, Ruth and Hester had by then married farmers' sons. Sister Alice, who was to remain a spinster, ran the household and was probably one of the reasons Jim did not marry until after she had passed away.

Jim Cook was the ideal neighbour and our joint boundary of at least one and a half miles of hedges, ditches and roadways never once caused a problem of any kind. Busy farmer as he was, he found time to captain the cricket team for twenty years. He was also a church warden and acted as MC at any functions in the Village Hall as well as being the Auctioneer at the sale of produce from the Harvest Festival.

After the war, in the autumn of 1945, together with Tom Bates, another local farmer, a game shoot was organised over the whole village and the proceeds donated to the Church for redecorating, something which had been neglected for many years. This shoot went very well and gave Jim the confidence to start up the 'Little Staughton Shoot' which is now in its 67th season and has given its members and guests many happy times.

Jim was seldom seen without his three companions, his pipe, his gun and his dog, the later of which, over the years he had several, none of them anything to write home about. The best one by far was a cross between a collie and a Labrador which, owing to an accident at harvest time, operated on three legs. This incapacity in no way hindered its progress and Jim taught it to run round the brussel field at first light to scare off the pigeons.

One foggy morning he went down to check on his gang of men riddling up potatoes when they were having their breakfast break. Jack Waller was one of them and his new false teeth had been giving him a bit of stick so he had taken them out and laid them on a sack nearby. The three legged friend, thinking they were a bone for him to eat, scooped them up and set off with Jack in hot pursuit and as they disappeared into the mist it must have been a bit like the finale of a Morecambe and Wise Christmas Show.

Dickie Reynolds
1876-1952
A True Son of the Pertenhall Soil

He was christened Daniel and lived with his wife Emma (née Mills from Easton) and three month old daughter Edith in a small cottage in Pertenhall according to the 1901 census where he worked as horse keeper for Joseph Bates at Wood End Farm.

Early in 1902 the family moved into another cottage with improved amenities near to the Moravian chapel. It was here that three more children arrived, Dora 1902, Amy 1904 and Jim 1906 which seemed to have filled up all the available space. In 1911 employment and a more spacious and modern cottage became available at Hoo Farm for Mr. Oliver which enticed Dickie to leave his job in Wood End Lane. It was all change about that time as in 1912 the Cook family moved into Hoo Farm and Dickie was promoted to cowman. More space in the home meant that Dickie and Emma could carry on with the breeding programme and six more children arrived at about two yearly intervals, Ivy 1914, Rhoda 1916, John 1918, May 1920, Albert 1922 and the tenth and last Gladys 1923.

As the school leaving age at that time was 14 years by the time Gladys was born it was most likely that her three elder sisters had left home to take up employment at one of the large local properties as servants. This was known as going "into service" and girls from what was known as "good working families" had no problem in finding jobs.

Having so many mouths to feed and only a miserly amount of money coming in, would have tested the resolve of the most resilient of characters, but what the indigenous working fraternity had in those days was a commodity that seems conspicuous by its absence in a high percentage of modern society and that is PRIDE and the get up and go attitude that we see in the animal world all around us.

Although Emma was a regular worshiper at the Moravian Chapel and actually paid a deposit so that she could eventually be buried in the tiny grave yard, Dickie was too busy with his work as cowman and gardening to take much part in religion or sport, as milking night and morning, weekends and bank holidays meant his tied cottage provided free accommodation for the family.

Dickie as well as cultivating his kitchen garden farmed three allotments bordering the road down Chapel Hill and on to the Way Post, which was nearly a mile round trip for him to travel and a bit further for the children to walk to and from school. He was knowledgeable as well as hard working and could quickly work out the tonnage per acre of the yield of crops on his allotments. Marrows were his speciality and tall stories abounded as to their size. The classic was that one of them on a Bank Holiday weekend grew across the road near the Post Office and the Bedford to Kimbolton bus had to stop for the driver to move it to the side. His ability to provide his large family with a constant supply of in season vegetables was a great help for Emma but of course meat is essential for the population in these northern latitudes to provide energy for the men to work and for children to grow properly. Local butchers delivered around the villages, but their products were quite expensive and Dickie found a cheaper alternative. He cycled to the Bedford market, late on Saturday afternoon, which was held down near the river bridge. A round trip of close on thirty miles, and it was similar to the farmers' markets we see in local townships at the present time. There would be several butchers in attendance and Dickie arrived at about the time they were packing up. In those days fridges and deep freezers had not been invented so good bargains were to be had by being in the right place at the right time and Dickie was able to buy enough meat to feed his family for the coming week for about half a crown which represented about one twelfth of his weekly wage. To keep meat from "going off" in hot weather a handy tip in those days was to lower a metal bucket containing the meat on a rope down the well just above the water line, the coolest place around.

Those reading this tribute, well over fifty years after his death could be excused for thinking he had a boring existence, but if so, they would be well wide of the mark. I can remember having conversations with him and was amazed at his knowledge of current affairs and how he would soon put the country right if he had the chance. He took great interest in his work and the running of the farm and was proud of the achievement of his large family who have all grown up and carried on the tradition of honesty, integrity and hard work.

There were, I feel sure, many parents in those days with similar credentials as those of Dickie and Emma who reared their broods without income support, baby bonuses, family allowance and tax credits but not too many whose offspring reached double figures.

Was it worth it?

"Time like an ever rolling stream bears all its sons away", the opening line of a popular hymn that packs so much empathy into very few words, especially when connected to someone we all knew.

Kelvin Newman after a long struggle with failing health passed away a short time ago and left a gap in our community that can never be filled. To see him trundling around delivering his wares on his push bike, it was hard to imagine that in his younger days his passion was hitting the trail on his souped up motorbike. The eulogy at his funeral service painted a comprehensive picture of his life and that of his family was most appreciated by the large congregation and a bit of an eye opener for many.

His constant companion was his fag and on days when there was a following breeze the aroma of a freshly lit gasper announced his imminent arrival. His father Stan was also addicted to the noxious weed, so it is no wonder the Chancellor of the Exchequer is having to cook up new ways of raising taxes. As well as the newsagents, Stan also ran a printing business and among other work also did the fixture cards for both the Cricket and Football Clubs, never sending a bill which was amazing as he was the only businessman in the town not to be one of over twenty Vice Presidents that ranged from Ron Atzema, the chemist, to Bill Whiteman, the Butcher.

During the time I was connected with the Cricket Club, one of my jobs was chasing the players up for their subs and taking the proceeds to the Treasurer Tom Pierce who was the Maths Master at KGS. I also delivered the Fixture Cards to the VP's, a bit time consuming, but rewarding, especially listening to the tales they told of times gone by. The secret turned out to be catching them in the right mood, not unlike farming and family planning.

One Friday just before lunchtime I called in at the garage, when

SV (Robinson) was doing up the wages so he said, "I may as well give you my cheque now." After thanking him I moved on next door to Bert Flanders, who wanted to talk about when the old Canon was the captain, and one Saturday in July 1930. "We were fielding when the fire bell sounded, so the Canon set off to man the Brigade, and as he walked past Bert at square leg he said "Take over the Captaincy now Flanders" and after a few steps he added "that is until I get back". The fire was at a thatched cottage up "The Hoo" in Pertenhall which was completely destroyed.

On my next visit to Tom Pierce, he said SV must be getting a bit absent minded, another cheque has arrived through the post.

The Canon's daughter, Evelyn was also on my list and after being plied with a liberal helping of sherry, sat back to hear about her early days.

"Instead of going to school I had a governess who lived in, a young French lady who I had to address as Mademoiselle and just on dusk one sultry summer evening, I decided to walk around the garden. As I approached the shrubbery, a strange noise attracted my attention and on closer inspection was shocked, so I ran to the house and said, "Father Father, come quick someone is trying to strangle Mademoiselle!" Later in life I realised she was not being strangled but Father took her to Bedford station the next day and put her on a train to Paris. Although the school master doing the "Strangling" never lost his job".

PS. The culprit who got lucky was not Tom Pierce, these fun and games happened long before he was born.

A Nice Surprise

Our small island, situated between several thousand miles of ocean on one side and an even larger land mass on the other, experiences changes of weather that are less predictable than in most parts of the world, with virtually any month being extremely wet or dry.

We have recently celebrated the 70th Anniversary of the miracle of the escape from Dunkirk when, had the weather been stormy, it could not have taken place. The German army had overrun the Low Countries and most of France in about two weeks, which prompted our history master, Mr. Owen, to devote our next lesson not on what happened in the past but what the future might hold for us. This was a very sombre forty minutes with invasion seemingly inevitable, but thankfully the weather and a few hundred brave sailors and fighter pilots saved the country and the rest of the world from Fascist tyranny.

Kyffin Owen, one of several Welsh masters recruited by William Ingram, was an amateur soccer international and was soon playing football and cricket for Kimbolton. He quickly became popular, especially when he married a local girl and was one of the first to explode the myth that it takes twenty years for a newcomer to become a native. His bride was Dorothy, daughter of Dick and Elizabeth Hall of the bakery, so they were soon on the guest list for party time at Manor Farm, Elizabeth, being one of Grandma's sisters. Grandfather got on well with Kyffin and was amused at some of his Welshisms that included "Yakky Da" instead of hello and "All Cerene" for cheerio.

The Owens lived in one of the school properties in front of the Castle Green and he went home to lunch on his bike and on the way back, went via East Street where Ladbrokes had a betting shop. His regular bet was a shilling each way and never wrote it out on a slip, just opened the door and said "Lucky Purchase" 2.30 Cheltenham or whatever followed by, "All Cerene". One day, the regular lady was away and a new girl took his bet and had been informed of the likely customers that might turn up. On the Saturday morning he called in to square up as most of his fancies had failed to oblige, and was surprised to be handed a pay packet the gist of which read "All Cerene" won the 4.30 at Nottingham at 20/1 and he had not knowingly had a bet on it.

Kyffin was one of those who put more in to life that he took out and well deserved his little bonus.

Characters of a Bygone Age

There were no lazy people around when I was a boy, you either worked or you starved. There was no in between and I am sure there were plenty of families who worked as hard as those that I knew. Of those, the Halls would have taken the biscuit, as well as having made them. Dick started work at 2 am and in July 1938 I was in quarantine at my Aunts with Scarlet Fever and my bedroom about twelve feet from the bakery. My clock registered 3.45am as I was awakened by a heck of a row going on outside. Dick's assistant, Neville Mash had arrived a couple of hours late. Baking tins, used as missiles, were being thrown around and the language far from parliamentary.

Dick's son Les lived just below Landins and ran a dairy herd in the meadows along New Town Lane. He would have had an impressive CV for as well as milking, night and morning he sold the milk around the town in cans hanging from his bike handlebars and in his spare time delivered the bread around the villages with his pony and cart.

His brother Stan, took a farm at Little Staughton and early on was short of equipment, so he asked his neighbour Bill Jordan if he could borrow his horse drag to clear up his hay field, but he proved unhelpful. Bill had perfected the art of eccentricity and it was said he would fall out with his own shadow if no one else was around.

His "bête noir" was his neighbour at Rectory Farm and he refused to attend the Silver Jubilee celebrations held there in May 1934. The next day Bill had a big party on his own farm with all his employees and their families invited, with events organised similar to those the day before and more drink and food on offer than could be consumed and every one going home with at least one prize.

Stan was also interested in greyhounds and with a like minded friend from Great Staughton had kennels built and a race track laid out in one of his grass fields. This really took off locally just before the war, particularly on Sunday mornings and enthusiasts instead of having to go to Walthamstow or White City for a flutter went to

Little Staughton and could spend their winnings at the Crown or Kangaroo on the way home to lunch.

The Party that Cost 200 Acres

Kimbolton has variously been described as either a village or a town, presumably by the teller, either to put it down or lift it up, perhaps it is somewhere in between. However, what is indisputable is that at one time it held a weekly market, with one side of the street the Sunny Side and the other, the Money Side. The Lion and George Hotels dominated the sunny side and both were coaching inns, complete with stabling. The landlord of the Lion, around the 1900's name was Hinsby and he also transported people to the other market towns and in the Pertenhall archives are photographs of the passengers alighting from his horse drawn bus at the crossroads.

Trade between the two inns was shared out fairly evenly, the football headquarters was at The Lion and Bernard Priestly, the landlord, was chairman of the club, when, just before WW11, it won both the Hunts Junior League and Cup in the same season. At the Annual Dinner, partying went on well into the night, with no breathalyser to worry about, the drink flowed freely. Whitemans, the butchers were close by and were very active on the sporting scene, which included a ladies hockey team. One member, Flo Hunt from Tilbrook, was quite a character and injected enthusiasm into those around her, a commodity that sometimes seems conspicuous by its absence in these more modern times. The Brass Band was also something to be proud of and performed at most functions, including the Kimbolton Grammar School Sports Day and neighbouring village celebrations.

The Cricket Club's headquarters was the George Hotel and the unlikely victory over the powerful Ramsey team in the 1947 Smith Barry Final precipitated celebrations to equal those of the football club a decade earlier. However, the landlady, Miss Gray, had noticed the Chairman of the St. Neots Bench was in the company and called 'time' at the appropriate hour. He then called an hour's extension to the license, an act that placed him on a higher level, than all his previous good works had accorded him.

Joe Hellett was one of the regular customers and although small in stature, was large in character and in his younger days, a useful jockey in point-to-point races. He was better known as a raconteur and the bigger the audience, the more unlikely the story, which was usually prefaced by "this is the Gods truth if I never lose this glass". Once, so carried away, he misjudged the distance between his hand and the mantelpiece and he dropped his glass in the fireplace!

Both hotel bars were well attended, with darts, skittles, various card games and dominoes, especially the double set that kept the standard of mental arithmetic at a high level. The stake was usually a pint or half pint of beer, but occasionally for a shilling, which was known as playing for a 'dry bob'.

The mid thirties, when Miss Gray arrived from the Wisbech area, coincided with the time when rural industries were at their lowest ebb and some customers had perfected the art of frugality to such an extent, their wives were said to have sewn their trouser pockets up. Miss Gray's car could have been filled up with petrol at either of two pumps in the High Street and five shillings would have bought four gallons – today's value 18 litres for 25p. The dining room was not part of the original building as it was accessed by a staircase from outside with the victuals arriving via a lift with rope and pulley cage from the kitchen below and any delay in serving was more than made up for by the quality of the fare.

Our farm shoot captain, not one to miss many tricks, booked our shoot dinners at The George and we were lucky that one coincided with Miss Gray's farewell party. Those of us who were not under curfew, joined in, thinking we were at Waitrose and were getting two for the price of one! One often hears about the 'party to end all parties' and this certainly was for the local medic, who, so carried away with festive cheer sang, 'The Ball of Kerimure' and failed to attend anymore shoot dinners. Another reveller not likely to forget was one of our shoot members, whose navigational ability did not match that of Christopher Columbus and his four mile journey home finished up, according to the signpost that read, Cambridge one and half miles. He eventually made it home around 4.30am where his wife, a conscientious lady, must have spent half the night making pastry as she happened to have the rolling pin in her hand which she used to part his hair and relieve him of his gun and us of two hundred acres of land from the top end of our shoot. But, as the French say, "C'est la vie".

A Salt of the Earth

When we were married in 1955 Dad had a house built for us on his land at Stonely. Smiths of Great Staughton did the work as well as about 50% of the building in this area at that time and were reckoned to be the most reliable operators.

Money was a bit tight then, but the price of £2,250 looks cheap today. This included a solid fuelled AGA complete with kettle, toaster and a selection of five saucepans with lids that came in at £125. Fred Hart who learned the trade working for Lynns at St. Neots, was the boiler man at KGS and serviced the AGA in his lunch time break, the cost 5/- or 25 new pence.

We were lucky as far as a baby sitter was concerned when our three children arrived at about two yearly intervals. Edith Presland and her husband Alf, who worked for a neighbouring farmer, lived only about a couple of hundred yards away across the fields so was able to turn up on foot. However, this meant crossing a rickety bridge over the River Kym, so if the weather was bad I ran her home in the car, a round trip of about three miles.

Eadie and Alf both came from large families, but they were not blessed with children, although she had the knack of knowing how to manage the newly born helping first time mums over that critical first few weeks. Later on she became the local 'Mrs. Mop' for several households in Stonely and Kimbolton. Alf was an enthusiastic gardener and grew enough veg to feed an army and Eadie distributed

Eadie Presland (Mrs P)

the surplus on her rounds on foot always carrying her shopping bag that appeared to be a permanent extension of her right arm.

She originated from Southampton, coming up this way just after Dunkirk when the south coast was evacuated as the threat of invasion became when and not if.

A maternity home at Paxton gave her the position of cook and later on she met Alf. They were an unlikely couple in the mode of Jack Spratt and his wife, with Alf always ready to grumble that his glass was half empty. Eadie on the other hand was chirpy and cheerful, her glass always half full, her slim line figure gave her speed rather than comfort and her willingness to help anyone to do anything anywhere at any time set her apart.

Alf was by and large a stockman and occupied positions where a tied cottage went with the job and worked on several farms before settling down in Stonely. For a time he was employed on our farm at Pertenhall and one Saturday morning in June 1948 Eadie came breezing into our kitchen just as I was getting ready to go on a farmers' outing to the Derby. She surprised me by asking me to put ten bob each way on one of the outsiders in the race.

The outing was organised by the NFU and on the way back the coach stopped off up the smoke for a slap up meal and a trip to the theatre. The star of the show was Alma Cogan, the raven haired Jewish singer who was fantastic, but tragically died of leukaemia a few years later.

The horse Eadie backed was "My Love" which romped home at odds of 40/1 so I was able to present her with five crisp white fivers. She deserved her bit of luck and later was able to spend her last few years at Newtown, Kimbolton in OAP accommodation where she became known as Mrs P.

Her memory will linger among the many to whom she devoted so much of her time.

Gone but not Forgotten

There has been a vast change in village life in the seven decades since the war, the main one being that every one is better off. Whether they are any happier is another question, but the old saying "Having plenty of money may not bring happiness but at least then it is possible to be miserable in comfort" is probably true.

The recent series of television programmes describing how life evolved billions of years ago were most interesting with some species, notably the dinosaurs among many others that have become extinct. This process is still ongoing with the number of old country characters in steep decline and at one time the village of Little Staughton had more per head of the population than any other of its size but where to start is a nice problem to have.

Hugh Pullen was an old bachelor who lived with his aunt in a desirable property set well back from the road near the top of Spring Hill. This provided a vantage point to see what was going on down below and a narrow bungalow with a chimney at either end he called "The Tunnel". After the war the Quenby family who farmed at the top end of the village started up a contracting business and the three sons were rushing up and down Spring Hill so often Hugh renamed it the "Inner Circle" and when any smoke was rising from chimneys at The Tunnel he said a train had called in to refuel.

As the son of a wealthy vicar he was left very well off, never needing to work for his living, but the downside was as a boy he became infected with TB and lost a lung in the process, which precluded him from service in the armed forces. Always known as Master Pullen rather than Hugh, probably stemmed from Feudal times when the Lord of the Manor's eldest son was heir to the Estate and thus the young master in waiting. He never owned a car and in the early days cycled to the Squash Club at Bedford to keep fit, but the lure of the pub finally got to him and towards the end he seemed to have embarked on a one man crusade to keep the brewing and tobacco industries in the right shape for future generations to enjoy.

Having had a good education he was intelligent, was the best of company in the pub never attempting to hog the limelight but was always ready with a one liner to raise a laugh. His assessment of someone who had passed away was that they had "Gone over the Rainbow", and when it was his turn to take that semi circular route he left fond memories for those who were privileged to have known him.

The Girl Next Door

As we grow older, every now and again, the phone rings bringing a message that a dear friend or relative has passed away. Just recently, we lost one of Pertenhall oldest inhabitants, whose life to so many was a light that shone brightly then gradually dimmed until the energy finally ran out.

Joan Gentle and her parents Mr and Mrs Peppit came to live as our neighbours at Chadwell End when she was about eight years of age and often played with my sister Stancy in a derelict cottage up the lane. It was known as Basses and had a thatched roof where the sparrows nested and one of the pastimes for boys in those days was collecting bird's eggs, now very much taboo.

On leaving school Joan went into service and during the war was at Bolnhurst Rectory when the BBC was evacuated from London to escape the Blitz and relocated to Bedford. Some of the top brass were billeted at Joan's place of work and one of her claims to fame was cooking breakfast for Alvar Liddell before he set off to read the 9 o'clock news.

In 1948 Joan married Ken and three years later son Allan was born and on growing up took after his father, being a talented cricketer, both as wicket keeper and hard hitting batsman at Kimbolton in 1970s when we won both the Millman 1st and 2nd XI competitions.

Joan supported all the village organisations and specialised in flower arranging and embroidery having infinite patience passing her skills onto those showing interest. She had that natural air of grace about her that cannot be copied or money can buy and the fact that the last dozen years of her life was blighted by injuries in a tragic car accident was sadness beyond belief.

During the well attended service in the church that was decked with floral tributes, Jean Tunstill delivered a moving eulogy of Joan's life, with Grant and Karen Williams hosting the wake at The Manor as caterers could not be found for it to be held in the village hall.

This brought back happy memories for me from when I was taken there in about 1930 by my grandmother to the church fete. The star attractions for children were the bran tub and Bonzo Caress' ice cream stall.

For the adults, clock golf on the lawn, tea and cakes with Kimbolton Brass Band filling the air with melodious tunes. General and Mrs. Lock were the hosts at that time and the villagers of Pertenhall must count themselves as fortunate to have residents like the Locks and Williams to give a helping hand in times of need.

CHAPTER EIGHT

Life is Like That

A Case of Mistaken Identity

The art of thatching has almost died out in these parts as most of the old properties that had that type of roofing have fallen by the wayside or been fitted with tiles.

Just a couple of generations ago, every farm would have had a competent Thatcher who would do the job on hay and corn stacks. The best materials were reeds from the fens but locally it was wheat straw with rivet wheat popular, as it grew taller than any other variety.

Alf Crissell, who lived in Little Staughton, became an expert and with his brother Charlie ran a good business thatching houses. This all came to a halt when he married Doris Fensome and her father gave them a small farm complete with house and buildings. Tommy Fensome was the top man at Colmworth running a steam engine business that specialised in timber hauling. He had a huge yard and workshops with mechanics to do his own repairs, so big in fact it was nicknamed Krupps Works after the German conglomerate that manufactured most of Hitler's Blitzkrieg equipment. Doris, always known as Doll, was the Company Secretary and although her marriage to Alf was not blessed with children they were very supportive of the villagers and gave presents to the OAP'S at Christmas or when they were poorly.

After the war, when farmers at last had enough money to enjoy sporting activities, shooting became popular and Alf soon became part of the scene. He ran the Colmworth Shoot and appeared as a guest on most of the neighbouring ones and was usually one of the first at the bar to buy a round of drinks. He always had a new joke to tell and when attending the Haulage Society Annual Dinner at the Corn Exchange in Bedford, the guest speaker failed to turn up. Alf got up and kept the assembled company amused for an hour and was probably better than the original choice.

When we grew vegetables, early potatoes were part of the plan, but as the weather warmed up they became difficult to sell and one of Alf's jokes was that the only two commodities in demand in August were ice cream and condoms, although he used the more romantic name for that protective equipment. Later on this joke became handy for me when I was trying to persuade our salesman at Brentford market to take a few extra tons. The salesman was banging on about lack of interest, owing to the hot weather and schools on holiday etc., so I quoted Alf's version of the only two things in demand at that time of the year. He replied, "We can't shift *them* nowadays because they are all buying these icebergs from Spain". He thought I had said fresh lettuce and the penny never did drop with him and helped to destroy the myth that the Cockneys were more on the ball than we mere lesser mortals.

Fun and Games Behind the Straw Stacks

The study of the origins of field titles would give an enthusiast plenty of ammunition to work with. Two fields at Little Staughton named 'Upper' and 'Lower Popes Hole' would be interesting to start with. Many are obvious and 'The Racecourse' on the left hand side of Sheridan's Hill is a case in point. This field was part of the Manchester Estate which was rumoured to have stretched from Norman Cross to Woburn, although there is no available evidence to support this story and may have been an exaggeration.

The bush telegraph indicated that at one time the in hand farm, at The Park, was profitably run and the Estate Office well in control of the situation until the slump in 1921, when the agricultural industry went pear shaped and the Wall Street Crash in 1929 sent it into a deep decline. Basically the bigger they were the harder they fell, with the Castle being sold in 1950 and the remaining land about 20 years later.

The racecourse was at one time good quality grazing land, but was neglected to the point that by 1939 it was a wilderness of pod thistles and ant hills, so large and numerous that it was possible to traverse the field by jumping from one to the next. There were a dozen or so stately oaks dotted about all over the field and permission to fell them was granted prior to bringing the land back into cultivation in 1940. A local farmer, who had obtained a licence to use explosives, came in to blow up the stumps. Unfortunately for him he forgot to read the instructions on the packet which stated *'after lighting the blue touch paper, retire to a safe distance'*. The huge explosion resulted in one of his thumbs being blown off and put him at a disadvantage rolling his cigarettes!

This was all in the days before the combine harvester, with crops first being cut by the binder and the sheaves stooked until dry enough to stack. Where there were fields any distance away from the farmstead, handy sites were found to save time and the little spinney bordering 'The Racecourse' was an ideal place and close to the road for the threshing tackle to approach. On the third or fourth harvest the crop was barley and the half dozen stacks had been threshed and the straw stacks left for cattle fodder.

One Saturday evening our gang was walking back up Sheridan's Hill, on our way home from a dance at the Mandeville Hall. As we reached the gateway near these straw stacks there was a strong smell of smoke and quickly flames spread through the stacks, when through the smoke came two figures each pushing a bicycle, one an American G.I. and the other an evacuee who was billeted at Pertenhall, with her husband away in the army and at that moment the most embarrassed person on the planet!

As they say, "all is fair in love and war" and in any case, a slice off a cut loaf is seldom missed!

A Prickly Subject

The general public have become almost immune to the shock of news that another organisation has succumbed to being on the fiddle. The Serious Crime Squad should be brought to account for failing to see the blindingly obvious, that when oil prices at the well peaked at 178 dollars a barrel about ten years ago, then recently fell by more than a third, the price at the pump is actually higher now!!.

Our morning paper has just been delivered by Max on his bike, the only vehicle not propelled by oil. Also our heating, the fertiliser and chemicals used on the farms are oil based so no wonder the cost of living keeps rising.

Quite what can be done about the Oil Companies rigging the price is out of our hands but rest assured they will wriggle out by some ruse trumped up by their legal teams.

The weather over this last twelve months has not helped to put much of a spring in our steps, but hope as they say springs eternal and by the time you read this the dog roses will be out and harvest just around the corner. Fingers crossed that the disease which ruined the wheat yield last year does not strike again or we will be up the creek without the proverbial.

Life of course was never meant to be that simple but it would help if the government were more in touch with the grass roots of the population. One of the unwritten rules that makes more sense than some of the waffle that emanates from government think tanks is that we should believe nothing we hear and only half what we see.

Just recently we have been told that the decline of the hedgehog population is due to climate change and loss of habitat, when we all know that it is the explosion of badgers that are the culprits and it is now illegal to disturb them.

Although the hedgehog could not in any shape or form be described as cuddly, they do clear up the odd million or two of slugs as well as unfortunately a few ground nesting birds' eggs.

Sixty years ago the local head keepers, Frank Cowland at

Kimbolton and Herbert Sygrove at Great Staughton, would have made sure this area was badger free and the dairy herds safe from TB. This disease is now spreading and is nothing to do with climate change or loss of habitat but loss of commonsense.

Yes, it is a Small World

I write this story having just had a three-week 'holiday' in Hinchinbrook Hospital, courtesy of the National Health Service.

Most people, unless they are very lucky, will at some stage find themselves looking at a strange ceiling in a ward with several other patients, some of whom may be in a worse shape. One of the old guys in our bay and about my age lived at Buckden as a boy and started working on a farm at the age of 14. He told the story of watching a dog fight between several Spitfires and a lone German bomber which was shot down over Eaton Socon in the summer of 1940. After twenty years on the farm he became a postman and on his bike delivered round four villages clocking up 26 miles each day, he certainly earned his retirement.

A couple of years ago my wife had a month in the same ward, but the difference now has to be seen to be believed with a wind of change having blown through. Everything seems more efficient and although some of the nursing staff may come from foreign lands and have difficulty with our language their smiles transcend all national boundaries.

The only member of staff to come into our bay who was less than welcome was the nurse, whose ultimate goal, it seemed, was to extract our blood samples with increasing frequency that made us think they had a secret colony of vampire bats with a thirst to match.

The food was the opposite of what hospital food has been branded in the past with a varied menu that even the most hard to please could find something to his or her liking. The only commodity I had difficulty with was the bread and came to the conclusion they used a little too much sawdust in the mix.

The surgeon Dr. Matthews who carried out my operation was a really nice person and explained everything that had happened to me, during my operation. He and his team visited each patient on their morning rounds helping to keep up their morale. Daughter Sally happened to be with me the day I was due to be discharged and as Dr. Matthews explained the things that would need to be done in my aftercare, he seemed to be very approachable, so I asked him if he played cricket at university. Yes, he had and years later, one of his sons actually dismissed Alistair Cook, the England opener, when playing for his school against Bedford School. My daughter Sally then mentioned that her three boys went to Bedford School, but were more interested in Rugby. Dr. (Mr) Matthews then said that another one of his sons played rugger for his university and by coincidence it appears that sometime during the previous season my grandson Harry had played in a Representative game and Mr. Matthew's son was in the opposition.

Something Missing

One of the consoling aspects of my stay in hospital was the fact that it was during the monsoon season and had I been at home on the farm I would have been tearing my hair out.

However, I did miss out on a good 80th birthday party but it was a small price to pay for coming back and being able to do most of the things I enjoy. One report to reach me suggested that the stack of empty wine bottles meant the guests had their drinking boots on.

At one time the success or otherwise of a party was directly proportionate to the number of cars that ended up in the ditch on the way home, but now with the breathalyzer, thumping headaches are just one legacy of over indulgence.

Our wedding in the mid 1950's coincided with at least half a dozen other farmers' sons getting married, and soon one of the most enjoyable forms of entertainment was the hosting and guesting at dinner parties. Some amusing stories have laid gathering dust in the archives of my mind that need airing before it is too late.

Protocol is more relaxed nowadays but at that time it was more "infra dig" to arrive early rather than too late, with the hostess having to juggle children's bedtime with preparing a hot meal. And so it was, we were due to attend the feast at a bungalow in the next village, but as we approached our destination, we saw the drive was empty, so we decided to whizz around the block and found we were in convoy with the other guests who were doing the same thing then we all drew in together.

Our turn came on a Friday, but when we got up in the morning, the Aga was stone cold, Claude had forgotten to stoke it up the night before. These cookers need at least 24 hours to reach full steam ahead so we went to our neighbours to see if they would cook the joint. Of course they agreed, but at lunch time it started to snow and by tea time traffic had ground to a halt and all the guests rang up to say they could not attend.

It's an ill wind that does not blow some good.

An old saying is that most things happen in threes, so the third event to come to mind where it was traditional to have roast beef with all the trimmings, except this time the Yorkshire pudding failed to put in an appearance.

Had it been nowadays, I would no doubt have dropped a hint that something was missing, as I have been known to wander along the path that angels fear to tread.

However, when the good lady hostess, who unfortunately is no longer with us, opened the bottom oven door to extract the apple pie, there sat the Yorkshire pud in all its glory.

Some Get Lucky

The saying "Old age does not come alone" just about sums it up for some of we elderly guys and dolls.

I seem to have a season ticket at Hinchingbrooke Hospital, for which I am extremely grateful and full of praise for the various treatments that have taken place. On one of my latest appointments for an X Ray I was loaded on a bed and propelled by a couple of nurses through seemingly miles of corridors and lifts and one sign with an arrow pointing to "Primrose Suite" triggered an impulse in my brain unlocking an old nursery rhyme we learnt at Primary School some eighty odd years ago that went something like this.

January brings the snow, makes our feet and fingers glow.
February brings the rain, which thaws the frozen lakes again.
March brings breezes, loud and shrill, to stir the dancing daffodil.
April brings the primrose sweet, scatters daisies at our feet.
May brings flocks of pretty lambs skipping by their fleecy dams.
June brings tulips, lilies, roses, fills the children's hands with posies.
Hot July brings cooling showers, apricots and gillyflowers.
August brings the sheaves of corn, then the harvest home is borne.
Warm September brings the fruit, sportsmen then begin to shoot.
Fresh October brings the pheasant; then to gather nuts is pleasant.
Dull November brings the blast; then the leaves are whirling fast.
Chill December brings the sleet, blazing fire and Christmas treat.

I well remember my three ops in the old Huntingdon County Hospital. How many wards there were I am not sure but ours had about sixteen beds, eight along each side with a wide gap down the middle. One op was to remove my varicose veins, after they were stripped out my legs were covered tightly with elasticated bandages which had to be left in place for three days.

As time wore on they became increasingly uncomfortable and sleep virtually impossible, however one night turned out quite amusing because it looked as though I could be a spectator in a love scene.

The orderly fancied his chances with the night nurse, but she kept telling him she was not in the mood. He kept persisting and saying it would be OK because no one would know, but I thought, "that's where you are wrong mate!" Whatever the outcome I am not sure, but had Sister Payne the hard bitten Matron got to find out she certainly would have had his guts for garters.

CHAPTER NINE

Village Life

The Case of the Disappearing Pubs

Since the beginning of WW11 the number of local pubs has more than halved and many varied factors can be considered responsible. The breathalyser and television come high on the list, but wartime conditions closed the Shoulder of Mutton and the Bushel and Strike at Little Staughton, leaving the Crown Inn to take up the slack. The large numbers of cars in the car park tell their own tale of the proprietor's success in attracting customers.

Keysoe only has one pub left out of five and one of the missing ones was the home of a wife and three daughters, whose husband was away in the RAF, a fact that did not go unnoticed by the Americans who were stationed at Thurleigh base just a bike ride away. Darts was the second most popular attraction and several dart boards must have been worn out between 1943 and 1945. The one downside of the game of darts is that someone is required to keep the score, known as 'taking the chalk'. In most pubs volunteers for this task were few and far between. There was never any shortage at that pub and one of the reasons may have been that the cloth for wiping the slate clean was actually a pair of…you've guessed it! However, the main thought in my mind at that time was not the beer and skittles or darts and knickers. I had just heard that Keith Webb, one of my contemporaries for five years at Kimbolton Grammar School, had been killed in a raid over Germany. We were the tiddlers in our class and he was the right size to be a rear gunner in a Lancaster bomber. There is a time to laugh and a time to cry.

Another favourite watering hole, not far away, which suffered a similar fate to many other thatched properties, was considered to be a little more up market than some of its rivals. This may have been due to two teenage daughters being in residence which helped to attract young bloods from far and wide, two of whom travelled in a new sports car whose exhaust was constructed to advertise its whereabouts. They kicked up a fair old racket on leaving the car park at closing time but pulled into a gateway down the road and when the coast was clear walked back, and prior information helped them to locate the gardener's ladder that reached up to one particular bedroom window. They must have been more miffed than the insurance company who had to cough up for the fire damage.

The inhabitants of Pertenhall should all now be honorary members of the Temperance Society, as at one time they had a choice of pubs to visit but now there are none at all. The first to go was the Bugle Horn, a thatched property down Wood End Lane. That burned down about the time of World War 1 allegedly struck by lightening. The cause was treated as suspicious at the time especially when shortly afterwards a pair of wealthy spinsters, who lived close by and were very anti alcohol, brought the license from the brewers so no pub could in the future open in the village.

The mid 1960's saw the second pub close its doors for the last time and its location, at a crossroads a mile from each of three villages, makes one wonder whether the person who chose the site was non compos-mentis. A delve into history proves otherwise. A local man, many long years ago, immigrated to Australia and was clever and lucky enough to come back with a small fortune. He had the pub built and appropriately enough named it 'The Kangaroo'. The odd location was to catch the passing trade that was avoiding the tolls in and around Kimbolton. It's an ill wind that does not blow someone some good.

From the 1930's onwards at least five tenants tried their luck at the Kangaroo. The first an old couple, whose son Jack played cricket for Pertenhall and was killed in the war which obviously put a damper on their proceedings. The only really successful landlord was Jabey Robins who kept the pub through the 1950's. Jabe was very

Outside the Kangaroo Inn around 1952
L-R: Claude, Joe Roddis, Jabe Robbins (the landlord), Hugh Pullen,
Charles Banks (Claude's father)

popular and knowledgeable of the countryside and local affairs and it was said that if Jabe didn't know about it, then it hadn't happened. His first job after moving in was to catch up about thirty homing pigeons that had bred unchecked in the outbuildings and were making a good old mess everywhere. He took them to St. Neots market, where to everyone's surprise, made a shilling each. After collecting the cash, he retired to The Canon for a celebratory drink or three. When he eventually returned home he was greeted by the sight of his flock of pigeons all sitting on the roof looking very pleased with themselves. The moral of this story is that after all, it is possible to occasionally to have your cake left, after it has been eaten.

A Thumbnail Sketch of Village Life in the Early 1930's

Pertenhall was a typical example in that 95 % of the population was wholly dependent on the soil and what could be grown upon it.

The farms were about half arable and half pasture as livestock were important for recycling by-products back to the land to maintain fertility. Horses were the motive power and crops like oats, beans and clover were the fuel that produced the energy. Every household had a large kitchen garden and more than 30 allotments were cultivated to keep a ready supply of cheap, fresh vegetables. On the largest farms the labour force would consist of a horse-keeper, a shepherd, several stockmen and enough general labourers to bring the total up to an average of one worker for every forty or 50 acres. Boys would start off as Saturday and Holiday boys at the age of ten years old so that by the time they left school at fourteen they were experienced. Several milking cows would provide income for the farmhouse. Butter would be made from the cream that was extracted from the milk by a hand operated gadget called a separator. So fresh cream, full milk, skimmed milk, butter and eggs could be bought from most farms. No need for shopping trips as butchers, bakers and grocers all delivered several times a week.

In the village there was a forge (blacksmith), a shop selling sweets and tobacco, a pub, a school, which doubled up as a village hall and finally a church and a chapel. The children walked to school and back home and again for lunch, no such luxuries as School dinners or family allowances. Old family members were cared for within the family circle and not bunged into old peoples' homes. Most folk had to walk or cycle, so no one was over-weight or needed fancy diet sheets to ponder.

The wage was about £1.50 new money for 48 hours per week and to make it easier to understand, the price of each of the following items could be bought for 5p (1 shilling).

30 Woodbine Cigarettes

3 pints of Beer

4 portions of fish and chips

3 loaves of bread

6 eggs

4 small pork pies or

8 jam Banburys from Halls bakery.

Religion played a much greater part in life than today with at least 75 % regular worshippers at Church or Chapel and Sunday work, except for stock feeding, was taboo. The Harvest Festival was probably the best attended service of the year. The Sunday before Harvest, prayers were offered for fine weather, but as you will see in other tales, this did not always go according to plan.

"Swotting up"

The archives at St. Neots Library have been very useful in helping me to verify facts and figures and it was whilst trying to track down how the village cricket team of Pertenhall managed to win the Shelton and District Cup in 1931 I stumbled upon one of the years when so many unusual happenings occurred locally.

As a small boy of five years I was at that time being brought up by my grandparents at Manor Farm, Pertenhall and can remember that at one time this mysterious thing called "Foot and Mouth Disease" was the main topic of conversation with the adults. Well it turned out that was 1931 and an outbreak at Spaldwick and four more at Chawston/Wyboston were too close for comfort, especially as farming and most other industries were in the grip of depression.

Also, it was the year that quite a severe earthquake occurred and I remember that at "The Elms", a large property occupied by several widowed and maiden aunts, a number of ornaments and a bottle of ink were dislodged from the mantelpiece in the sitting room and lay broken on the floor.

A real gem however was a detailed account of a massive Fayre held at the Castle to help raise £1,000 for church repairs. This runs to 75cm (2.5ft) of column inches and a Photostat copy is available. The names of over 140 local people are mentioned as helpers and what their duties were.

This helps to demonstrate the mysterious thing called "community spirit" has been around a long time and not something that Hitler invented for us.

Local Memories: A tale from the days gone but not forgotten.

The small village of Shelton tucked away in North Bedfordshire would probably be more accurately described as a hamlet, but what it lacks in size is more than made up for in its history, quite a large proportion of it by the Whitehead family. William Senior, a wealthy Irishman, came over in about 1870, bought most of the village and set up residence at Hall Farm. His aim was to establish a stud to breed racehorses mainly for steeple chasing and winning the Grand National, his ultimate goal. There is no doubt that money was no object in his quest for The Holy Grail and he was not the first nor will he be the last to fail to realise his dream, the best he achieved was second with "Detail" in 1903. However, he cleaned up most of the prizes at the Bedford and Huntingdon Races and was one of those responsible for planning the course at Kimbolton, where one of his horses "The Curate" won the first and the last race on the card of Monday April 18th 1892.

His wife produced a son for him in 1881, also named William, who became a day boy at Kimbolton Grammar School during its decline and after a few years he went on to board at Wellingborough Grammar School where academic standards were regarded as the best in the UK.

By the time he was twenty he was training horses on his own account, but at Newmarket, and had broadened his sporting horizon to include boxing and cricket. Both he and his father were over six feet tall and he would have been a formidable opponent in the ring. He started up boxing clubs in Rushden and Northampton and provided financial as well as moral support for many youths whose talent he had unearthed and for the less able an interest to keep them out of mischief.

His love of cricket led him to turn one of the horse meadows into a playing field and in 1921 started up the Shelton and District

League. Seven other villages were invited to take part and he donated a cup for the winners of the league in a match at the end of the season at Shelton. This was a red letter day with the Whiteheads supplying free tea for everyone and as much beer as could be consumed by all and sundry. Unfortunately the competition petered out in 1931 with Pertenhall the last winners and Mary Roddis still having the cup in safe keeping.

Fact finding missions to pinpoint the reasons for its decline are thin on the ground, with very little from the archives to help. Of the eleven years the competition ran, Dean were winners six times, but when the Rushden League started up in 1930 with promotion and relegation an added encouragement, their first team joined it and left their second team in the Shelton League, otherwise they may well have won it twice more. Another reason may have been that in 1931 Foot and Mouth disease had broken out at Spaldwick and Chawston. All the pitches would have been in fields with grazing livestock and the farmers would not have been keen to add to the risk of spreading the disease by allowing matches to take place.

Hall Farm (like all others employing half a dozen men or more), brewed their own beer to be handed out during the busy seasons of hay time, harvest, thrashing and sheep shearing, those with less men paid them extra at those times which was known as "beer money". Modern times have seen this culture progress to bonuses, so large that thick heads would have resulted had this been given in alcoholic drink.

One of the amenities the village lacked was a pub, so in 1915 the Whiteheads, always supportive of the villagers, had one built and named it "The Cat and Custard Pot", probably straight from a "Jorrocks Annual". Another unusual aspect was it was sited bang on top of the main footpath – no doubt so that it could catch all the passing trade.

Point to Point Racing

The sport of hunting, like that of shooting, is a by-product of the farming industry, both taking place when land work is at its lowest ebb. Every hunt has its own territory and towards the end of each season, holds a steeplechase meeting, known as a Point to Point. 'The Oakley' is our local hunt and it has had at least ten different locations for its races. The first available evidence is that it was held at Cow Bridge, Bedford in March 1880, followed two years later at Kimbolton and copies of three of the race cards from that era make interesting reading. After enjoying the latter site for twenty-five years the Committee came under pressure to move somewhere more central and the change of ownership of Hoo Farm, Pertenhall, (which provided half of the circuit) probably precipitated the move to Wilden, Stagsden and Turvey, in quick succession, before the advent of World War 1 ended the fun and games for quite some time.

The hunting fraternity is without doubt the most resilient of any organisation and did not need the events of the past decade or so, to prove it. The bloodlines of some of these hardy souls, go back to ancestors involved in cavalry charges through enemy lines and if their point to point venue has to be changed, so be it. Just pack a map and compass, with the hip flask and 'Tally Ho'.

After a brief period at Chicheley, at the end of WW2, the era of nomadic existence ended when a home, for fifty years, was found on Jim Harris's farm at Newton Bromswold. Many willing hands erected permanent buildings which together with superb parking and viewing facilities attracted large crowds and most of the top competitors, including 'Spartan Missile' and 'Oxo', who both went on to win the Grand National at Aintree.

During the period between the two World Wars the meetings were held at Risely, where a three and a half mile circuit was constructed that crossed Swineshead Road twice before an uphill finish sorted out the men from the boys. This may have been one

HRH Edward Prince of Wales Point to Pointing

of the reasons that in 1928 it was allocated the most prestigious race in the Point to Point calendar, 'The Brigade of Guards Inter-Regimental Challenge Cup', ridden by members of the Armed Forces. These races always attracted a good turnout of local spectators which swelled to an estimated five thousand, when news broke that the heir to the throne, Edward, Prince of Wales, was to be one of the competitors. He was known to have been a 'bit of a lad' and swarms of females barred his way, at every turn, hoping to catch his eye. His mount was the favourite of the 25 runners but it unseated the Prince half way round, which suited the bookies who had taken a bit of stick in the earlier races.

During the proceedings, which included Tom Gifford riding a winner and Joe Hellett getting third in the farmers' race, the loudspeakers announced that pickpockets were active, but too late for those who had already been relieved of their 'readies'.

The Second World War resulted in most of the course going under the plough and the local rabbit population finding winter oats a nice change from grass. In those days farm workers were allowed to go rabbiting as one of their perks and so it was that a group were ferreting round the old racecourse. One set of burrows needed the help of a spade which unearthed half a dozen folded pieces of leather, the remains of the empty wallets the pickpockets had hidden all those years ago in case they were searched on the way out of the point-to-point meeting. Yes, there were villains even in the 'Good Old Days' but it makes a change from reading about old ladies being mugged for their pension money.

Up with the Lark

April brings the primrose sweet and scatters daisies round our feet, so the old nursery rhyme goes. This year it also brought an extra Bank Holiday to celebrate the Royal Wedding, which takes me back to the things that happened in May 1937 for the Coronation of King George VI and Queen Elizabeth when we were also given a holiday.

On that day a number of messages of good luck were ferried across the country by relays of boys to end up at Buckingham Palace. The weather that day was perfect with unbroken sunshine and as I awaited soon after day break at the top of Hornsell Hill, the boundary between Pertenhall and Swineshead, regaled in my white PE outfit for the scroll to arrive I felt ten feet tall and not the four foot six of pent up energy. The mile and a half to the Kangaroo was

Fancy dress at Pertenhall Cricket Field for George V Jubilee, May 1935

Claude's Grandmother "the Bride" and Jim Cook "the groom". Joe Roddis and Jim Clark the "black and white minstrels" and Claude a boy scout at the front with the lop-sided hat.

covered in record time and handed over to Sid Saunders to do the next leg to Bushmead Cross. Sid was a bit older than me but also at KGS and sadly among many others who were to give their lives with the RAF in WWII.

The afternoon celebrations included a fancy dress parade at the cricket field and a treasured photograph reveals Grandma Banks and Jim Cook as bride and groom first prize with Joe Roddis and Jim Clark runners up as the Black and White Minstrels among many other entrants. Later on a cricket match, ladies versus the gents who had to bat and bowl left-handed, was predictably won by the ladies, not the first time nor will it be the last contest to be fixed by umpiring decisions.

An evening meal in the barn at Manor Farm ended proceedings when several barrels of beer were consumed which loosened the tongues of the singers of old songs that have sadly disappeared into the mists of time. The country had for some time been without a monarch as after King George V had passed away his eldest son the Prince of Wales was due to be crowned King Edward VIII. However, he was a bit of a lad and did not choose his lady friends in the manner appropriate to his position. He was currently in a liaison with an American divorcee and a furore developed concluding with a hastily arranged Cabinet Meeting which decided that Edward should either give up his latest bird or relinquish the throne. He decided to choose the second alternative which shocked the nation and delayed the Coronation for about a year.

This gave plenty of time and ammunition for the scribes who are clever at constructing amusing and sometimes ribald verse elbow room to perform. One such missive started thus

"There was a young fellow named Ted

Who took Mrs. Simpson to bed"

Sorry chaps I have run out of space probably a good thing or all the maiden aunts I meet in the High Street will look the other way.

Behind the Lace Curtains

The small village of Swineshead is probably the least spoilt of all and the woods that can be accessed up the lane behind the Church are a joy to visit. Beauty is said to be in the eyes of the beholder, whether a picture of an unmade bed in the Tate Gallery, or of the sun going down on Galway Bay, but for my money the view of the bluebells in flower in Swineshead Woods takes a bit of beating.

A few years ago when the woods came up for sale they were snapped up by the Woodland Trust and now can be enjoyed by the many and not just the few. Such is the range of hedgerow and wild flowers, throughout the season the pollinators are kept busy, until hibernating for the winter to emerge again in the spring for the cycle to be resumed.

The village has not changed that much since I first wandered through in about 1933 and bought some sweets in the shop kept by Mrs Nicholson, who together with her husband were natives of Chelveston and after their wedding in 1921 came to live in a cottage in Church Lane. Evie the first of a brood of seven came along during the two years at their first home. They were then able to buy a larger house in the centre of the village and had a bit of luck when the GPO advertised for someone to start up a Post Office and they were the successful applicants. Shortly afterwards they opened the shop which kept going for thirty years. With plenty of space now available the breeding programme resumed with Stan, Grace, Edna, June, Gordon and Gwen, making the sound of tiny feet slightly more than just a patter. Now only Edna is left in the village to fly the flag for a "once upon a time" role model family.

In those days the village boasted at least five farms and several small-holdings which employed all of the men folk. Now the work is done by one farmer, employing one regular man, with a bit of extra help at harvest time. Not many people nowadays would like to swap places with Mont Measures, one of those small holders whose bike had more miles on the clock than most. He pushed it along as he walked his cows to graze in a field at Pertenhall each morning in the summer time and then rode it back home and at tea time did it in reverse to bring them back for evening milking.

In the Autumn when the daylight decreased his cows stayed at home and his yearlings taken to the field in Pertenhall and foddered up each day with a truss of hay carried piggy back style kept in place with a pitchfork as he cycled along, and the field ever since is known as "Monts".

Timothy Bletsoe, an eccentric old bachelor, lived with his two spinster sisters in the Old Rectory and his passion was hunting with "The Oakley". He exercised his skewbald horse each day, often coming past Pertenhall School when we were out at morning playtime. He was always immaculately dressed as if he was going to a meet with riding hat, white gloves and boots that were shone up like mirrors. The strange thing about the set up was that he was never on the horse's back but walking along the road leading the horse on the verge and probably finished up being fitter than the horse. An old Yorkshire saying has it "There's nought so queer as folk," maybe some of his ancestors came from that county.

A Happy Hunting Ground

Every village, within a comfortable bike ride of Pertenhall, has provided a wealth of memories that thankfully, advancing years has (up to now) failed to dim. Born into a farming family during the 1920's depression I was soon made aware that silver spoons were in short supply and a list of jobs to do before and after school were the norm rather than the exception. Fortunately sporting genes had percolated my DNA which enabled me to make many friends at cricket and football as well as in business. Now with ever increasing frequency some of these old mates are called to higher orders as was the case recently at Hargrave, the home of Ralph Gilbert.

Mere words cannot adequately describe the esteem in which he was held by those privileged to have known him, and a whimsical smile that flickered across his face greeted every one. Hard grafting and skilful with whatever machine he was charged, occupied most of his working life. Beginning with the Gyrotiller during the war and later with a bulldozer, quarry levelling and increasing field sizes this meant that livestock farming became uneconomic. His hobbies included motor bike racing in the early days, and later as a foot follower of local hunts. His marriage to Joan was blessed with the arrival of Graham followed by twins, Geoff and Yvonne with Denise and Jon completing a nap hand, so manpower had to replace horsepower, tending the garden to produce a supply of vegetables to feed the growing brood and many prizes were won at Flower Shows, putting the icing on the cake. The church service included well known hymns and the large congregation responded by attempting to arouse from their hibernation any bats that occupied the belfry. Welcome refreshments in the village hall were well received and sent my mind back to just after the war, when our gang of boys found Hargrave Village Hall to be "Mecca" as the American Airmen had left behind a useful supply of pretty girls. Quite why there were no boys around to spoil our fun may have been the new water supply, affecting the gender of the next crop of babies but 'it is an ill wind that does not blow some good'.

"Socials" were popular in those days but success depended on the wit of the MC and at Hargrave, Edwin Smith had it off to a fine art. Fund raising was one of the objectives and occasionally items were donated to be auctioned to increase the kitty, the most unusual of which was a cream-maker. A jug shaped vessel that held about a pint of milk with a handle that operated a whisk, add a knob of butter or margarine turn the handle for a minute and "Hey Presto" a jug of cream, a delicacy in those days of rationing.

Is it now gathering dust on a shelf somewhere? Has it been to the Antiques Road Show? However, if by chance Ivy, Gwen, or Pat have it in safe keeping I would like an invitation to inspect the same as "I shall soon have to be ready for that long, long sleep, when my mind makes appointments that my body can't keep."

An Apple a Day

We are fortunate in this area to be so well served by the NHS. The multiple staffed Medical Centre in Hunters Way, Kimbolton and Great Staughton Surgery. This is a far cry from when I was a boy and Dr Ellis coped on his own with Kimbolton and the surrounding villages, helped by Phyllis then Gwen, his daughters, who acted as receptionist cum nurse mixing and dispensing medicines in their spare time. Dr Ellis had come down from London in 1929 to assist Dr. Robinson after Dr Dean had passed away and was able to hit the ground running because he knew the lie of the land having spent a week here as a locum the year before. The wording of the telegram that alerted him "Dean dead, come at once" suggested that he was aware he would be called upon at some stage and all went well until Dr. Robinson died suddenly in 1938 leaving Dr. Ellis to cope on his own until 1945. All three doctors had lived in turn at the property in the High Street that is now the Old Swan Pharmacy their home being the surgery that spanned more than a century in time.

The second WW saw a transfusion of new blood into the area in the shape of the Royal Army Medical Corps who took over the Castle. Several of the soldiers married local girls. One of them, Tommy Granger, married Phyllis in 1942 and on demob joined his father in law in his practice and became Dr Granger, later on having a house built in a field at Pertenhall and planting it up with Cox Orange apple trees, to give him an interest away from the daily grind.

By the early 1950's Dr Ellis had about worn himself out and Dr. Kilby, another ex service man was drafted in to take his place. Together with Dr. Granger, their partnership blossomed as they continued the service that the previous doctors had established, with the telephone being manned 24 hours a day seven days a week and a surgery at Risely twice a week and visiting patients over an area of more than 30 villages.

As with every successful enterprise, there is someone behind the scene pulling the strings and in this case it was Iris Mumford whose hand was on the tiller for 42 years, and was known to the doctors as their "Girl Friday", and in 1984 she helped to organise Dr. Kilby's retirement party in the Lewis Hall. This was without doubt the "Do of the Decade" with the guests being wined and dined in time honoured fashion at the end of which in his speech, after thanking everyone for coming he recalled some of his most interesting experiences saving the best until last.

Receiving a phone call late one Sunday evening, in the midst of a raging blizzard, from a local farmer saying that the daughter of one of his workmen, who lived in a cottage a mile up an unmade road, was in distress and he was to go to the farmhouse and he would be taken to the cottage in the Land Rover. After a hair raising journey across the fields they arrived at the house and the doctor was ushered into the girl's bedroom. Shortly after he came down and reported the mysterious illness was solved and a baby would be born very shortly.

The mother was shocked at the news and said it could not be true as her daughter never had a boy friend. The doctor explained they were not now living in Biblical times and she must have been in a man's company at some stage. Soon a noise from the bedroom like that of a hare in a snare was the baby announcing it's arrival and Dr. Kilby came down into the kitchen and asked for a towel to dry his hands and was given the cloth off the birdcage that was doubling up as the budgerigar's night shade.

This was a fitting end to Dr. Kilby's dedicated career, and when the dust had settled it later transpired that the girl was in the habit of visiting the local pigeon shooter in his hide.

So this story lends weight to the old adage that one of the reasons so many take part in country sports, is not so much about what they get, as what they might get.

The Jolly Boys Outing

We shall soon be celebrating the 67th Anniversary of our farm shoot, during which time we have used at least a dozen local hostelries for our dinners. This last decade we have been extremely well fed and watered at The Chequers in Keysoe, and it is many happy returns for me as this is the place Snowy, my best mate and I as well as most of the Pertenhall lads cut their drinking teeth.

Saturday evenings were about the only time many could afford that luxury and most of the company were men who worked on local farms. Darts was the favourite pastime with the reigning champions, Ebin George and Bud Ruff putting everyone to the sword. The first part of the evening revolved around discussions of

Boys Outing to Skegness

L-R: Tony Shelton, Arthur Stapleton, Claude.

(Note all smoking!)

what was happening on the farms with Ebin and Bud, who worked on a big farm at Thurleigh, which specialised in growing potatoes, holding court. During the autumn, potatoes were lifted and stored in clamps and pits as they were known and every Saturday we had to listen to how many hundred yards the pit had lengthened and visions of it extending like a modern day Hadrian's Wall into the North Sea a distinct possibility.

For the darts, the best of three sets of 301 up, starting and finishing on a double were the rules and a half pint to each of the winners kept the show on the road. The game kept the standard of mental arithmetic at a high level, with most being able to subtract 67 off 123 or whatever, as soon as they took the darts out of the board and after

Ebin had thrown, he could often say "tops left, Bud". Silence reigned as Bud made his way to the ochie mostly with a freshly lit Woodbine that his tongue manoeuvred back and forth across his lips, like the windscreen wiper on a Morris Minor whose battery was on the blink. "Plonk" the first dart in the double 20, game over.

After the war ended in 1945 thoughts of enjoyment started to take the place of austerity and someone at the Pub suggested we went on a bus outing to the seaside. Such was the interest the ability to fill a train let alone a 26 seater coach looked likely, so yours truly volunteered to organise. Peter Woolston agreed a price of £8 for the round trip to Yarmouth which together with a couple of crates of beer to lubricate the tonsils for the sing along on the way home meant collecting 6/6d or 32½ new pence from each one.

Life is one long learning curve and it was my first experience of trying to extract money from those whose enthusiasm vanishes "like dew before the sun" where handing over cash is concerned. With a week to go the number was stuck on 20 and I almost wore out a set of tyres on my bike looking for the rest – I managed just one. The day arrived with unbroken sunshine and as we piled on board Peter announced that the only seaside with amusements open on a Sunday was Skegness, so off there we went.

Just recently, Arthur Stapleton has presented me with a photo of us together with Stan Dawson, Tony Shelton and others walking along the promenade all smoking cigarettes. The irony for me was that everyone I met in the weeks afterwards said, "If you had asked me I would have loved to have come with you." Anyway if there are any readers still alive and kicking who made the trip, please get in touch so we can rendezvous once again at "The Chequers".

Downhill All The Way

By the time this epistle sees the light of day many readers will be wondering what the weather will be like for the outdoor celebrations of the Diamond Jubilee.

The day of the Coronation in 1952 was one the coldest June days in living memory, with an overcast sky and constant drizzle that enveloped everything in its path, putting at risk the brass monkey's ability to reproduce the species. For the farming community the decade of the 1950's was a depressing time with three wet harvests and some of the older ones who experienced the pre-war slump beginning to fear the worst.

The gradual drift of farm workers away from the land accelerated at this time, with many going to Ferrersflex at Newton Bromswold a labour intensive project that manufactured synthetic leather products for the booming car industry and were able to offer much higher wages. The combine harvester had by now replaced the binder which brought a new head ache with what to do with the harvested grain that was too damp to store and was a problem our Dad could have well done without. He had always seemed happiest when working with his flock of sheep. It was obviously in his genes of which fortunately, I have not been afflicted.

And so it was that Bank Holiday morning after a leisurely breakfast, Dad and I set off to check the livestock round the farm. The first stop was the field up Swineshead Road to creep, feed the lambs, who together with their mothers, were huddled up near the three portable hay racks that were still full and had been for the last month, but by the next morning had been cleaned out, the ewes preferring stale hay to wet cold grass. Then on to Hoo Farm where the yearling cattle and a few single suckler cows were grazing, then on to the land at Stonely before heading to the Metropolis for a lunch time drink.

The George Hotel was well attended and a free glass of sherry to each of the customers was a nice gesture from Roger and Eileen Dunkley, the new Managers. After a couple of pints someone said that a race down the High Street at 3 o'clock was open to all comers, which was good news for me although an hour in the pub and a large lunch not the ideal preparation.

Over thirty competitors turned up and were split into two

groups; I was among those running second. The start was at the war memorial so downhill with a following wind I had no problem in breasting the tape and went in to the final with a dozen or so others. However, I had to be content with second place to a young RAF bod who ran in the first heat and had the benefit of a ten minute breather.

My prize was a five shilling voucher that could be redeemed at any shop in the High Street. The fact is that I never did spend it and over the years it has disappeared into the mists of time, meaning that compound interest on 25p over sixty years should help the traders weather the next financial crisis.

And Finally…

We have been brought up on "Dad's Stories". Many is the time Dad says, "Did I tell you about the time when…" etc etc. and the thought bubble in your head says "yes, at least 100 times" – but of course you say, "no, I don't think so"… "Well it was like this…" and away he would go again!

I am thrilled that we have managed to get the stories down on paper and still Dad is writing – who knows – a second volume!

I have never "published" a book before and would not have managed without the help, advice and support from Gareth Thomas and Sue Bolton. Trying to place a story in a particular chapter, when, for example, there has been a massive *thunderstorm* at a *school cricket match*, during the *Second World War* – has been challenging but fun.

Thanks also to Francis Frith for permission to use the 1900 Map of Pertenhall, also to Photocare of St Neots for making very old photographs and newspaper cuttings into the good quality pictures you see in the book.

I am enormously proud of our Dad. He has battled illness for several years, at the same time as nursing our mother, who is also in poor health. But Dad's memory is still as sharp as ever and long may we be treated to his stories of years gone by.

Penny Young

The author at his 88th Birthday Party in Fancy Dress